Learn Computer Programming
with the Commodore VIC

Lionel Carter is a qualified Chartered Mechanical Engineer and Principal Lecturer in Management Science at Slough College of Higher Education.

Dr Eva Huzan is Head of the Computing Division at Slough College of Higher Education, a member of the Computing Science Advisory Panel ('O' and 'A' level), University of London, and a committee member of the British Computer Society Microprocessor Specialist Group.

Learn Computer Programming
with the
Commodore VIC

L. R. Carter
M. Tech., C. Eng., M.I.Mech.E., M.B.C.S., F.O.R.

E. Huzan
BSc., Ph.D. (Physics), Ph.D. (Computing), F.B.C.S.

HODDER AND STOUGHTON
LONDON SYDNEY AUCKLAND TORONTO

First printed 1982

Copyright © 1982
L. R. Carter and E. Huzan

British Library Cataloguing in Publication Data

Carter, L. R.
  Learn computer programming with the
  Commodore VIC.
  1. VIC (Computer) – Programming
  2. Basic (Computer program language)
  I. Title   II. Huzan, E.
  001.64'24   QA76.8V/

ISBN 0 340 28070 0

Printed and bound in Great Britain
for Hodder and Stoughton Educational, a division of
Hodder and Stoughton Ltd, Mill Road, Dunton Green,
Sevenoaks, Kent by Richard Clay (The
Chaucer Press Ltd, Bungay, Suffolk.
Photoset by Rowland Phototypesetting Ltd,
Bury St Edmunds, Suffolk.

Contents

Acknowledgements

We would like to thank Commodore, especially Andrew Goltz and John Baxter, for their helpful advice and assistance.

List of Figures

List of Tables

Introduction

The Commodore Colour VIC computer has many facilities which you can use for a variety of applications in the home, at school, in offices and laboratories, wherever you have a mains point and a television set.

As soon as you switch on your VIC, you will have access to the BASIC programming language; BASIC stands for Beginners All-purpose Symbolic Instruction Code. You will be able to write useful programs in BASIC very quickly by working through this book. No knowledge of computers or programming is assumed and the many exercises and problems (with answers in the appendices) will help you to progress at your own speed.

An attractive feature of the VIC is its colour capability. You will learn about colour and easy-to-use animation techniques early on in the book so that you can introduce these facilities in any of the programs. The VIC also allows you to program a variety of sound effects. Sample routines are given in this book which you can include in your own programs.

The versatility of the VIC is demonstrated further by the sections on high-resolution graphics, which do not require any special program packs although you will need an extra 3K RAM pack. All the subroutines necessary to produce high-resolution graphs are given in this book.

The applications dealt with in this book include:

colour effects, animation and high-resolution graphics;
sound effects and Morse trainer;
cost calculations and mortgage calculation;
stock file processing and simulation;

processing scientific and engineering data;
simple and more complex mathematical calculations.

These by no means exhaust the types of applications for which you can use the VIC. Once you have mastered these simple applications you will be able to start using your VIC for more sophisticated tasks. For example, the user port on the VIC can be used to control models and scientific equipment. You can obtain further attachments for your VIC, such as joy sticks and paddles for games and control applications, and a disk unit and printer for more advanced business applications.

1 Introduction to Computers and Programming

1.1 Basic functions and units of a computer

An essential function of a computer is the ability to store the set of instructions required to process a particular task. This set of instructions (the *program*), which is prepared by a programmer, has to be held in the computer's store (its main *memory*) while the instructions are followed.

Each computer has a fixed instruction set which it can execute. A *control unit* selects the instructions, one at a time, from the memory, decodes or interprets them and causes the computer to carry out the instruction. If the instruction requires an arithmetic operation to be performed then the control unit transfers the necessary data between the memory and the *arithmetic and logic unit*.

The main memory, arithmetic and logic unit, and control unit comprise the central part of the computer, and together are known as the *central processor*.

Input and *output* peripheral devices, linked to the central processor, are used to insert programs and data into the computer's memory and to output results from there. Typical input devices read and decode patterns of punched holes on cards or paper tape, or sense marks optically or magnetically, and transmit this information electronically to the central processor. Alternatively, the information can be keyed in directly from a keyboard (similar to that of a typewriter). Results may be displayed on a television screen or visual display unit, or, if a 'hard' copy is required, printers are available which print either one character or a complete line at a time across a page. Graph plotters may also be used as output peripherals.

Programs may be stored magnetically on *backing* or *secondary storage* devices, and these can then be read back into the computer's memory when required. On large (mainframe) computers, magnetic disks and tape are used for this purpose, while on the smaller microcomputers the equivalent devices are floppy disks and cassettes which hold less information and transfer it much more slowly. Other forms of secondary storage, such as magnetic bubble memories, are also available.

Secondary storage devices are also used to hold files of data records. These are transferred to and from the computer's memory under program control for file processing applications.

Figure 1.1 shows the basic units of a computer, the flow of data and control links.

1.2   How information is held

A computer is largely made up of a number of two-state devices. The 'off' state of the device may be considered to represent a 0 and the 'on' state a 1. A numbering system comprising only 0s and 1s is called a *binary system*. Different patterns of these binary digits (or *bits*) may be used to represent a character set and ranges of numbers.

Numbers are represented in the computer's memory as a combination of bits. The number of bits available to represent a number varies with the computer used. When using BASIC, most systems will work in floating point arithmetic, in which numbers are held as a *mantissa* and an *exponent*. For example, $6 \times 10^3 = 6000$, has a mantissa of 6 and an exponent of 3.

1.3   Programming a computer

Each family of processors has its own instruction set which is likely to differ from that of other processors. This means that a particular processor is only capable of understanding its own set of instructions in *binary code*.

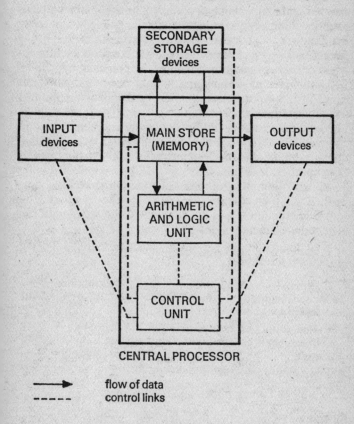

Figure 1.1 Basic units of a computer

The computer's memory can be considered as consisting of a number of cells capable of storing binary patterns representing program instructions or data. Each of these cells is uniquely numbered so that reference can be made to particular memory cells, either to select a program instruction or data, or to write data into a certain memory cell.

As an example of how programs are written in a computer's own code (machine code), it will be assumed that two numbers are held in memory cells 5 and 6, that these are to be added together, and the result stored in memory cell 8. The addition will be performed in a storage location called the *accumulator*, so the first instruction needs to load one of the numbers into the accumulator. The second instruction adds the other number to the number in the accumulator, which will then contain the sum of the two numbers. The third instruction stores the contents of the accumulator in the required memory cell.

The binary codes for these instructions for a typical processor are shown in Table 1.1

	Instruction	*Machine code*	
1	Load number held in memory cell 5 into accumulator	10100101	0101
2	Add number held in memory cell 6 to number in accumulator	01100101	0110
3	Store number held in accumulator in memory cell 8	10000101	1000

Table 1.1   Machine code instructions

In one program run, memory cells 5 and 6 could have been set to 70 and 25, respectively. After the three instructions in Table 1.1 have been obeyed, cells 5 and 6 would still contain 70 and 25 and cell 8 would now contain 70 + 25 i.e. 95. The same program could be run again with different data in cells 5 and 6 (say 43 and 12), which would result in cell 8 having its previous value of 95 replaced by the new value of 55.

1.4 Programming languages

As you have seen, programming in the computer's own machine code requires that the instructions and data are given to it in binary. Writing down and keying in a series of 1s and 0s is time-consuming and prone to error. An alternative way of expressing the instructions is to use *mnemonic codes*. For example, the command to load a number from a memory cell could be written as LDA instead of, say, 10100101. Also the memory cells could be given symbolic names instead of referring to them by their actual numeric (binary) addresses.

This type of programming language is used when it is necessary to have close control over the functions of the computer. Languages which use such mnemonic codes are known as *assembly languages*. Each assembly language instruction usually corresponds to an equivalent machine code instruction. The translation of the assembly language program into machine code is carried out by a machine code program called an *assembler*.

High-level languages have been devised which allow several machine code instructions to be expressed in one statement. BASIC is such a programming language as shown in the example below:

$$LET\ C = A + B$$

is a BASIC statement which causes the two numbers, held in memory cells called A and B, to be added together and the sum stored in memory cell C. This is the same problem which previously required three machine code or assembly language instructions.

However, neither assembly language nor BASIC programs can be understood directly by the computer. BASIC programs need to be translated into machine code using a *compiler* or *interpreter*. The basic difference between these two is the stage at which the translation from BASIC into machine code is performed. Using a compiler, the translation is done *before* the program is executed; this gives speed advantages over an interpreter which performs the translation process as it executes the program. The VIC BASIC interpreter is particularly suitable for first-time users because it has been designed so that programs can easily be altered and corrected.

1.5   Microprocessors and microcomputers

The development of microtechnology has opened up the use of computers to many more people than was previously possible, and has changed the way many applications can be handled. In addition, the compactness and low cost of microcomputer-based systems are making possible new applications.

Microelectronic devices (integrated circuits) are made from wafer-thin pieces of semi-conductor material, such as silicon. A small chip of silicon, a few millimetres square, can contain a very large number of electronic components built into circuits.

Integrated circuits (ICs) which have a wide variety of processing and storage functions are available. Today it is possible to have all the circuits needed for a microcomputer on a single semi-conductor chip, which is about the same size as the early ICs that contained only a few components. Large Scale Integrated circuits (LSIs) contain many thousands of components.

In a microcomputer, the chip performing the functions of the central processor is called a microprocessor. The microprocessor performs the following functions:

Synchronisation of processing events and instruction decoding (control unit);
Temporary storage of addresses and data (registers);
Arithmetic and logic operations (arithmetic and logic unit).

Further information is given in *Microelectronics and Microcomputers* L. R. Carter and E. Huzan, Teach Yourself Books, 1981.

Your VIC contains Commodore's own 6502 microprocessor and another Commodore special-function processor: the video interface controller. The video interface controller inside your VIC is a special microprocessor which controls the colour and sound signals output to your television set. It contains special control registers which you can change under program control.

2 Simple Input and Output Statements

2.1 READ, DATA, INPUT and PRINT statements

This chapter explains how you may enter information into your VIC computer (*input*), and how the VIC may be programmed to supply information, for example on a printer or video screen (*output*).

Each BASIC instruction (or statement) consists of a command to the computer to carry out a certain action, and a combination of variables, constants, separators (e.g. a comma) and operators (e.g. +) on which the action is to be performed. For example:

10 READ A,B,C

tells the VIC to read three numbers (numeric constants) from the DATA statement (see line 20 below) and store them in three cells in the VIC's memory identified by the names A, B and C. A, B and C are called *variables* and refer to unique numeric addresses, as explained in Chapter 1. When A, B or C are referenced again in the *same* program, the VIC will obtain the current contents of these cells. In a *different* program, A, B and C may refer to cells with different actual numeric addresses but unique for *that* program. Single memory cells are referenced in BASIC programs by single letters of the alphabet, A–Z, followed optionally by a single number, 0–9, or another letter A–Z.

The 10 before READ in the statement above is the *line number*. Line numbers enable you to change particular lines in your program by retyping the line. Gaps may be left in the sequence of line numbers for subsequent insertion of additional instructions. Three further instructions complete the program to read and output (PRINT) three numbers:

```
20 DATA 25,11,30
30 PRINT A,B,C
40 END
```

The END statement terminates execution of the BASIC program, i.e. the processing of the program instructions is stopped.

Note that the following three statements have the same effect as the above READ statement. That is, after these three instructions have been executed with the DATA statement shown in line 20, A, B and C will contain 25, 11 and 30 respectively.

```
10 READ A
11 READ B
12 READ C
```

Type this program into your VIC exactly as shown, pressing the RETURN key once at the end of each line. After the complete program has been typed in, type LIST to check that this has been done correctly. If there are any mistakes, you can 'edit' the program by moving the cursor to the required position. There are special cursor control keys which allow you to move the cursor to the left and right and up and down. Once you have reached the position of the mistake on the screen, simply type over the mistake with the corrected character. After the correction has been made, press the RETURN key with the cursor still in position over the line which is being modified. On re-listing the program, the corrected version should appear on the screen.

To help you in editing, there is a special insert/delete key which allows insertion of spaces and deletion of characters. The LIST command can be used to list a particular line (e.g. LIST 30) or groups of lines (e.g. LIST 200–250).

When you have entered your program correctly, type in

the command RUN and press the RETURN key to initiate execution of your program.

Note in particular how the contents of A, B and C (i.e. 25, 11 and 30) are output and the number of spaces between the numbers. Change the program so that the PRINT statement is as follows:

30 PRINT A;B;C

and note the spacing between the numbers when a semi-colon is used to separate the variables in a PRINT statement instead of a comma.

To change the data, you will need to alter the numbers in the DATA statement. Alternatively, you may use an IN-PUT statement instead of READ and DATA statements. Replace the READ and DATA statements in the program by the following statement:

10 INPUT A,B,C

(delete line 20 by typing 20 and pressing the RETURN key). When run, the VIC will output a question-mark (?) to indicate that data should be input from the keyboard.

A heading may be output at the beginning of the output from the computer by putting it in double quotation marks in a PRINT statement as in the following example:

28 PRINT "A", "B", "C"
30 PRINT A,B,C

(*Note*: In computer codes the *same* character is used for open and closed double quotation marks.)

An alternative method of identifying the three numbers is to output A = followed by the number. Experiment with the following statement to obtain the spacing you require (delete line 28):

30 PRINT "A =";A; "B =";B; "C =";C

The information in the double quotes is output as given in line 30, while A, B and C which are *not* in quotes refer to memory cells. If A, B and C contain 25, 11 and 30 respectively, line 30 will output:

$$A = 25 \quad B = 11 \quad C = 30$$

You may put extra spaces ($\triangledown$ indicates a space) between the quotation marks. For example, substituting,

$$\text{``}\triangledown\triangledown\triangledown\triangledown\triangledown A\triangledown = \text{''}$$

in statement 30 above would result in A being output with five spaces before it and one space before the equals sign.

The TAB function may be used to output information in particular column positions on your video screen as illustrated in the following example:

30 PRINT TAB(3);"A =";A; TAB(10);"B =";B;TAB (16);"C =";C

This will cause A = to be output in positions 4, 5 and 6, followed by the contents of cell A, then B = in positions 11, 12 and 13, followed by the contents of cell B, then C = in positions 17, 18 and 19 followed by the contents of cell C.

The TAB function will be discussed further in subsequent chapters.

2.2 String variables

For many problems it is necessary to input, store and output variable information which consists of a mixture of letters, numbers and special characters, including spaces. Such a series of symbols is called a *string*. Strings may be stored in *string variables*. These must be given a name consisting of one of the alphabetic letters A–Z (followed optionally by another letter A–Z or 0–9), followed finally by a dollar sign \$, e.g., A\$, B\$, C\$, . . ., Z\$.

The constant information given in double quotes previously is termed *a string constant*.

String variables are essential for reading in and manipulating files of information, particularly for business applications. Just a few examples of the use of string variables are given here to give you some initial practice.

Once a program has been written and proved correct, it may be used over and over again with different data, on different occasions and by different people. It is useful, therefore, to output the date the program has been run, and perhaps by whom. Two string variables may be used to input this information and to cause it to be output.

Change and insert statements in the program to output three numbers as follows:

        10 INPUT A,B,C,D$,N$
        26 PRINT
        27 PRINT "DATE   ";D$;" ";N$
        28 PRINT

When this amended program is run, in reply to ? you will need to input three numbers separated by commas (for A, B and C), followed by the date and your name. For example, input data for the above program could be:

        ? 25,11,30, 26/08/81 , J.SMITH

Try running this program with different data, different dates and your name. Notice that the PRINT statements at lines 26 and 28 output blank lines.

2.3   Obtaining the required print layout

It is important to design suitable output so that this can be output in different formats for different purposes. Various ways of using name and address information will be used to illustrate this. The program given in Table 2.1 inputs a title (MR, MRS, MISS etc.), a name and an address, so that this is stored in memory cells referenced by string variables, and outputs a letter heading, notebook label and envelope label.

The six INPUT statements shown in Table 2.1 will cause the computer to request six lines of data to be input. When

```
10 INPUT T$
20 INPUT N$
30 INPUT A$
40 INPUT B$
50 INPUT C$
60 INPUT D$
61 PRINT"□":REM CLEAR
70 REM LETTER HEADING
80 PRINT TAB(3);A$
90 PRINT TAB(3);B$
100 PRINT TAB(3);C$
110 PRINT TAB(3);D$
120 PRINT
130 PRINT
140 END
150 REM NOTEBOOK LABEL
160 PRINT
170 PRINT
190 PRINT"*********************"
200 PRINT
210 PRINT
220 PRINTTAB(5);N$
230 PRINT
240 PRINT
250 PRINT"*********************"
260 PRINT
270 PRINT
280 END
290 REM ENVELOPE LABEL
300 PRINT
310 PRINT
320 PRINT
330 PRINT TAB(5);T$;" ";N$
340 PRINT TAB(5);A$
350 PRINT TAB(5);B$
360 PRINT TAB(5);C$
370 PRINT TAB(5);D$
380 END
```

Table 2.1 Name and address program

working interactively, each line of data is entered in response to the ? output by the computer as shown in Table 2.2.

Enter and run the program on your VIC. Save the program on cassette by typing in SAVE"TABLE 2.1" and press the RETURN key; the VIC will then prompt you.

The REM (remarks) statements at lines 61, 70, 150 and 290, in Table 2.1, are only listed with the program to explain the program's actions. Note that you can put more than one statement separated by a colon (:) against one line number (as shown in line 61). This avoids using extra line numbers and is shown in several examples in this book. The 'clear screen' character, shown in quotes in line 61, is obtained by pressing shift and the CLR/HOME key. This will give you a clear screen so that the letter heading is displayed at the top of your screen. When the END instruction is reached at line 140, execution of the program is terminated but you can continue the processing by typing the command CONT, and similarly at the end of the 'Notebook Label' part of the program to continue after line 280.

> ? MR
> ? J. SMITH
> ? 1 THE AVENUE
> ? LONDON W8
> ?
> ?

Table 2.2 Data for program

The notebook label will contain just the name of the owner in between two lines of asterisks. However, at this stage you will not be able to centralise the name, according to its length, for names of varying length. This will be dealt with in Chapter 5 as an example of the use of test instructions.

If you have worked through this chapter step by step, you

should be able to answer all the following questions. Test yourself referring to the appropriate sections in this chapter if necessary.

2.4 Questions

1 Explain what a variable is in BASIC.
2 Which command did you use to run your BASIC program?
3 How did you change an instruction in your BASIC program?
4 How did you delete an instruction in your BASIC program?
5 How did you insert an instruction in your BASIC program?
6 If your VIC outputs a single question mark (?) during the running of a program, what does this indicate?
7 In which positions are numbers output on your VIC when there are *commas* between the variables in a PRINT statement?
8 In which positions are numbers output on your VIC when there are *semicolons* between the variables in a PRINT statement?
9 How are string constants represented in BASIC?
10 What are string variables and how may they be used?
11 What is the purpose of the TAB function? Give an example.
12 What is the purpose of the REM statement?

3 Arithmetic Operations

3.1 Constants and variables

Your VIC may be programmed to perform a variety of calculations by means of arithmetic assignment statements in which the result of the calculation is assigned to a memory cell. For example:

$$50 \text{ LET S} = X + Y$$

causes your VIC to add the contents of memory cell X to that of memory cell Y and puts the result in a memory cell called S. X and Y will have had values assigned to them previously, either by an INPUT or READ + DATA statements or by another LET statement. The contents of cells X and Y are unchanged by the action of the LET statement. For example, Table 3.1 shows the contents of X, Y and S before and after execution of the above LET statement, in a program which contains the following statements in addition to line 50 above:

$$30 \text{ READ X,Y}$$
$$40 \text{ DATA 123,56}$$

Cell	Before	After
X	123	123
Y	56	56
S	?	179

Table 3.1 Contents of X, Y and S

Note the original, unknown, contents of S has been over-written by the new value 179, the sum of 123 and 56.

The variables on the right-hand side of the equals sign in a LET statement may be operated on by a number of different arithmetic operators, and may be mixed with constant values (constants). For example:

$$51 \text{ LET I} = \text{I} - 1$$

subtracts 1 from the current value of I, so that after the LET statement has been obeyed I has a value one less than its previous value. Note that the word LET may be omitted.

The *numeric constants* that may be used are:

a) whole numbers (*integers*) which do not contain a decimal point, for example, −45,360 (or +360);

b) numbers containing a decimal point (*floating point*), for example, 8.123, −97.5;

c) numbers in exponential format, for example, 12.3E4, which represents $12.3 \times 10^4 = 123000$ (4 is called the exponent). The exponent may also be negative, for example, 12.3E −4, which is $12.3 \times 10^{-4} = 0.00123$.

Note that numbers are made *negative* by putting a minus sign (−) in front of them; a plus sign (+), or *no* sign, indicates the number is *positive*.

Any number that is used in the program, either as a constant or as the contents of a variable, must lie within the range limits of your VIC i.e. ±1.70141183E+38, ±2.93873588E−39 for largest and smallest numbers, respectively.

3.2 Arithmetic operators

The symbols on the right-hand side of the equals sign in a LET statement may consist of variable names, constants and arithmetic operators; this combination of symbols is called an *arithmetic expression*. The *arithmetic operators* indicate which arithmetic operation is to be carried out on the numbers in the arithmetic expression. The following list shows the order in which operations are performed unless changed by the use of brackets as explained in the next section.

Arithmetic operators	Meaning
↑	raise to a power (exponentiation)
*, /	multiply, divide
+, −	add, subtract

3.3   Hierarchy of operations

It is possible to use brackets in an arithmetic expression to give the correct meaning. The contents of the brackets are evaluated first starting with the innermost pair of brackets and working outwards. For example, to evaluate

$$\frac{5 + 9}{4 + 3}$$

the top line (*numerator*) needs to be added first, then the bottom line (*denominator*) needs to be added, and finally the numerator is divided by the denominator. Brackets are used to ensure this order of evaluation.

A program to illustrate the order of evaluation is given in Table 3.2; the larger gap in the sequence of line numbers

```
30 READ B,C,D,E
40 DATA 5,9,4,3
50 LET A=(B+C)/(D+E)
70 PRINT B;C;D;E;A
80 END
```

Table 3.2   Program to illustrate order of evaluation

between the LET and PRINT statements will allow the insertion of additional statements later. Table 3.3 shows the contents of the memory cells before and after the LET statement in line 50 has been obeyed.

Cell	B	C	D	E	A
Before	5	9	4	3	?
After	5	9	4	3	2

Table 3.3 Contents of B, C, D, E and A

Run this program on your VIC and then amend the LET statement as follows (i.e. remove the brackets).

$$50 \text{ LET } A = B + C/D + E$$

A will now be 10.25 (i.e. $\frac{9}{4}$ + 5 + 3). This is because the VIC evaluates the arithmetic expression in a certain order if there are no brackets, depending on the arithmetic operators in the expression.

If there are no brackets, then the VIC will perform the exponentiations first (if there are any), followed by multiplication and division of equal hierarchy, but in the order left to right, lastly addition and subtraction of equal hierarchy. Within brackets the same order of evaluation is carried out, innermost brackets being calculated first as previously stated.

Looking again at the last statement at line 50, you will see that the division, C/D, has been carried out first as it is of higher hierarchy than addition. This gives a completely different result from that calculated in the previous LET statement in Table 3.2 where brackets were used.

3.4 Arithmetic expressions and statements

Insert all the LET and PRINT statements shown in Table 3.4 into your program and run it. Output all the results

```
50 LET A=(B+C)/(D+E)
51 LET G=C/E-B*D
52 LET H=C/(E-B)*D
53 LET J=G-H/E+E↑2
61 LET S=C*D-B↑A
62 LET T=(C*D-B)↑A
63 LET U=(E*(C-B)↑(D/A))
70 PRINT
71 PRINT
72 PRINT"B=";B;"C=";C;"D=";D;"E=";E
73 PRINT
74 PRINT
75 PRINT"A=";A;"G=";G;"H=";H;"J=";J
76 PRINT
77 PRINT
78 PRINT"S=";S;"T=";T;"U=";U
80 END
```

Table 3.4 LET statements

(A,G,H,J,S,T,U) together with the variable names as identification. The data read and the final results are shown in Table 3.5.

$$B = 5 \quad C = 9 \quad D = 4 \quad E = 3$$
$$A = 2 \quad G = -17 \quad H = -18 \quad J = -2$$
$$S = 11 \quad T = 961 \quad U = 48$$

Table 3.5 Data read and final results

Notes

1 Line 51 could be replaced by

$$51 \text{ LET } G = (C/E) - (B*D)$$

to give the same result, although the brackets are unnecessary in this case.

2 The brackets in line 52 are essential to give the correct answer, as can be seen by comparing the results of line 52 with that of line 51.

3 In line 53, H is used in the expression because a value was assigned to it in line 52. Instead of E↑2, you can

use E*E which is a quicker operation. Amend line 53 to

$$53 \text{ LET } J = G - H/E + E*E$$

and check that you get the same result for J.

4   In line 61, B↑A (i.e. 5^2) is evaluated first, then C*D (i.e. 9×4) before the subtraction (i.e. $36 - 25$) is carried out. However, in line 62 the contents of the brackets are evaluated first (i.e. 21) before this is squared by A.

5   There are three pairs of brackets in line 63. The innermost pair is evaluated first from the left, that is, C − B (equals 4), then D/A is evaluated (equals 2). The exponentiation is carried out next to give 4^2, and finally this is multiplied by E (i.e. 3).

```
51 LET G=C/(E-B)*D
52 LET H=C/(E-B*D)
53 LET J=((G-H)/E+E)↑2
61 LET S=C*(D-B)↑A
62 LET T=C*(D-B↑A)
63 LET U=E*C-B↑D/A
```

Table 3.6   Changes to arithmetic expressions

As a further exercise, change the arithmetic expressions in lines 51–63 in Table 3.4 to those given in Table 3.6. Check your results with those given in Table 3.7. Your VIC has the facility for changing individual characters in a line; use this facility instead of typing whole lines again.

B = 5 C = 9 D = 4 E = 3
A = 2 G = −18 H = −.529412 J = 7.97232
S = 9 T = −189 U = −285.5

Table 3.7   Results of arithmetic operations

3.5   Problems

You are now ready to attempt some simple problems. For more complicated problems, it is advisable to express the logic in the form of a *flowchart* before coding it in BASIC, as explained in Chapter 4.

In your programs, use constants instead of variables for values that are not going to change during the execution of the program or from one run of the program to the next. Variable names should be meaningful: for example, use E for Expenses.

Write programs and run them on your VIC for each of the following problems. If you get errors, reading Chapter 4 will help you to correct them. Compare your programs with those given in Tables A1 and A2 in Appendix A; substituting actual values in place of the variables will help you understand the action of each instruction. The output from each program for the data given is shown in Tables 3.8 and 3.9. You should experiment with a variety of PRINT statements to give different outputs, e.g. underline answer with hyphens or asterisks, line up values.

Problem 1 – Number of £s required

On your proposed visit to the USA, you will need 150 dollars a night for accommodation and 125 dollars a day for

```
LENGTH OF STAY:
  5 NIGHTS
ACCOMMODATION:
$ 150 PER NIGHT
EXPENSES (MEALS ETC.):
$ 125
ALLOWANCE (PRESENTS):
$ 100
EXCHANGE RATE:
  1.75 ($ TO THE £)

£ REQUIRED
  842.85
*******
```

Table 3.8 Output from 'Number of £s required' program

food, travelling and incidental expenses. You intend to stay
five nights and wish to take sufficient dollars to have 100
dollars to buy presents. How many pounds sterling will you
need to exchange if the exchange rate is 1.75 dollars to the
£ ? (Your program should be flexible enough to cope with
changes in expenses, the length of stay and the exchange
rate for subsequent visits.)

Problem 2 – Cost of stationery

Calculate the cost of stationery for a course that is being
run, given the following information:

Number of delegates attending	58
Cost of folders	14p each
Cost of paper	26p per pad
Cost of pens	12p each

Allow two pens per delegate (there is a quantity discount of
8% for orders over 100 pens). Write the program so that it
may also be used on other occasions, when different numbers of delegates will be attending, and allow for changes in
costs.

NO OF DELEGATES:
  58
COST OF FOLDERS:
  14 P EACH
COST OF PAPER:
  26 P PER PAD
COST OF PENS LESS 8 %:
  12 P EACH

COST OF STATIONERY =
£ 36.00
****

Table 3.9 Output from 'Cost of stationery' program

4 Program Development

4.1 The need for pre-planning

This chapter gives you guidance on developing a proposed program. If a program is written too hastily valuable time may be lost subsequently in implementing the necessary changes. Time spent pre-planning is seldom wasted. Commercial systems designers and programmers are expected to conform to a specific formal procedure. In developing your own programs, you need to exercise self-discipline.

4.2 Understanding the problem

The first step is to ensure that you understand what you intend or are required to do. Are the terms of reference clear? This might mean that you need to check the meaning of any terminology or jargon used. You may also need to ensure you understand the mathematical notation used to specify any relationships involved. Thus, initially, some research or background reading may be necessary. Research may also be necessary when you know what you want to do, but are not sure of the method to be used.

4.3 Designing output

The starting point of designing a program should be the output. You need to consider and make decisions on the following aspects.

The output from a program may be printed and/or written to a file. Is your output going to be solely printed, written to a file or a mixture of both? This leads on to deciding precisely what is to be printed and what is to be written to the file.

For example, your intention may be to write a program to read a stock data file and produce a list of items to re-order. Given, for the moment, that a program can be written to identify the items to be re-ordered, you need to consider: should the output be solely a printed list or should a re-order file be produced that can be the input to a purchase order program? If you are going to have a printed list of items to be re-ordered, what should it contain? Should it list the complete stock record of each item or, the other extreme, should it just be a list of stock code numbers?

A program of this nature is developed in Chapter 11, in that case the re-order list consists of stock code and stock description. The whole record was not printed but only sufficient to fully identify each stock item.

Having decided what is to be output it is then necessary to consider the format and general layout. The considerations to be made are:

In which columns are the variables to be printed?
Should they be truncated or rounded?
Are column headings necessary?
Are main headings necessary?
What spacing is required between headings?
Should headings be underlined?

The output to a re-order list program might therefore start as shown in Table 4.1.

```
40 PRINT"RE-ORDER LIST"
45 PRINT"-------------"
50 PRINT
60 PRINT"CODE";TAB(7);"DESCRIPTION"
65 PRINT"----";TAB(7);"-----------"
70 PRINT
```

Table 4.1   Headings for re-order program

4.4 Input requirements

Once the output details have been decided you can then identify the necessary input. If a large amount of data is to be processed it may be advisable to read it from a data file; this is dealt with further in Chapter 11. If the data is solely associated with the one program it can be incorporated in DATA statements, while data that varies from run to run is best entered via INPUT statements.

You may not be the only person using the program and this is a factor to be considered. Values should be entered in their most usual form, i.e. 12.5 not .125 for interest rates (see, for example, the mortgage problem in Chapter 12). Ample print messages should be provided, giving guidance, if necessary, as to the input required.

A further aspect of the input design is the desirability of providing some form of control over the program during run time. For example, in the 'Heat of combustion' problem (Chapter 12), the user is asked whether any more data is to be processed and replies Y or N, i.e.

```
100 PRINT "ANY MORE DATA"
105 PRINT "(Y = YES, N = NO)"
110 INPUT Y$
```

4.5 Flowcharting

Once you have a broad idea of your requirements the logical sequence of the program statements needs to be developed. This can be done by drawing a flowchart. The more common symbols used in flowcharts are shown in Figure 4.1

An example of the use of the flowchart symbols is given in Figure 4.2, where it is required to calculate the average of three numbers. The purpose of a flowchart is to ensure the logic is correct before becoming involved with the detail of individual program statements. Further examples of flow-

Symbol	Use

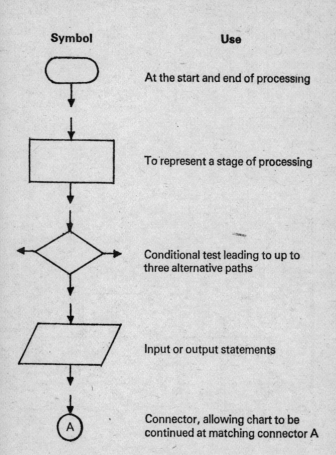

At the start and end of processing

To represent a stage of processing

Conditional test leading to up to three alternative paths

Input or output statements

Connector, allowing chart to be continued at matching connector A

Figure 4.1 Some flowchart symbols

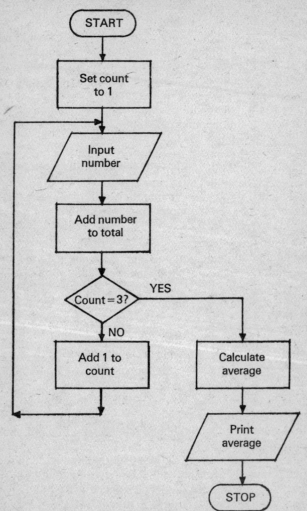

Figure 4.2 Flowchart for average of three numbers

charts will be found elsewhere in this book accompanying the descriptions of programs.

On occasions it becomes apparent from the flowchart or analysis of the problem that a similar calculation will be repeated several times in the program. When a similar set of program statements is likely to be required in several parts of the program, this may indicate the possibility of writing them once only as a *subroutine* and using this routine several times over. A discussion of subroutines is the subject of Chapter 9.

Having drawn flowcharts, the next stage is writing the program. When the program has been written, you still have not finished. A very important part of producing useful programs is to ensure that they perform as intended, and the next section discusses the testing and documentation of your programs.

4.6 Program testing

If you make a mistake in the use of the BASIC language, your VIC will detect this and output a message to tell you that there is a *syntax error* in your program. Examples of typical syntax errors are: mistakes in spelling (e.g. IPUT instead of INPUT), wrong instruction format (e.g. LET $X+Y=S$ instead of LET $S=X+Y$), unacceptable variable name (e.g. 2A instead of A2). You must clear all the syntax errors before you proceed.

Your program may still be incorrect after the syntax errors have been cleared. You may get an *execution error* caused by asking your VIC to perform an action which it cannot do. For example, if values are calculated by your program which are either too small or too large you will get arithmetic overflow (this will happen when dividing by zero). An execution error will occur also if you try to assign a string to a numeric variable (e.g. using D instead of D$ for a date, 26/08/81).

A program which runs successfully, without an execution

error occurring, may still give the wrong results because the logic of the program is incorrect. You should work through your flowchart and/or program instructions with typical data before running the program on your VIC (this is known as performing a dry-run). Then run the program on your VIC with this typical data; this should be designed to test every instruction path in the program (i.e. every branch in your flowchart).

It is important to write down details of the program and its use, for subsequent reference. You will find it useful to include the following sections in your documentation: Identification, Contents Page, Summary, Description of the Problem, Specification of the Problem, Input and Output Formats, Use of Program, Interpretation of Outputs, Modifications, Appendices.

5 Conditional and Unconditional Branching

5.1 Controlling the order in which instructions are obeyed

For most problems your VIC needs to be programmed to *repeat* a set of instructions and to execute different sets of instructions in the program according to the requirements for that particular run. This is done by means of *branch* (jump) instructions.

The GOTO instruction causes control to pass to the line number in the statement. That is, the computer will execute next the statement it has branched to and continue to execute the instructions following in sequence until it encounters another branch instruction. For example:

```
50 LET I = 1
60 PRINT I
70 LET I = I + 2
80 GOTO 60
```

will cause the odd numbers 1, 3, 5 etc. to be printed. When the computer executes the instruction at line 80, it will always branch to line 60 and obey that instruction followed by line 70. Therefore, the GOTO statement is an unconditional branch instruction, since it is always executed independently of any condition that exists.

However, you will notice that in the above section of a program, there is no instruction which stops the program being executed; it will go on for ever!

To stop the computer executing this set of instructions, you will need to insert a conditional branch instruction. This will perform a test to see if a condition exists and pass control to a different part of the program according to the result of the test.

A conditional branch instruction that you may use in BASIC is the IF . . . THEN statement. For example, to stop the program which prints odd numbers, you could add the following instructions to those given above:

$$65 \text{ IF I} = 21 \text{ THEN } 90$$
$$90 \text{ END}$$

Try running the program and see if it stops after 21 has been printed. If you replace 21 by an even number, say, 20 or 22, the program will not stop since I never has this value.

5.2 Loops and their control

This small program that you have just tested has a set of instructions, lines 60–80, which are performed repeatedly, thus forming a loop. The flowchart for this program shows the loop and the branch out of the loop more clearly (see Figure 5.1). Notice the GOTO 60 instruction is represented by an arrow from box 70 to box 60.

There are several alternative ways of exiting from a loop and for branching to different parts of a program. The format of the IF . . . THEN statement is:

line number IF *relational expression* THEN *different line number*

Notice that the line number following the THEN *must* be different from the line number preceding the IF, otherwise the IF statement itself will cause continuous looping.

The relational expression is the test that is to be performed. If this test is true (that is, the condition exists), then control passes to the line number following the THEN. If the test is false, then control passes to the line number following the IF statement, that is, the instructions will continue to be obeyed in sequence until another branch instruction is met.

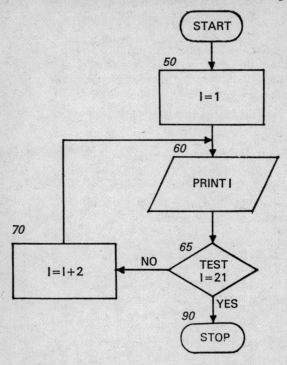

Figure 5.1 Flowchart to illustrate loop control

The relational expression compares two expressions, so that its format is:

expression relational operator *expression*

You have already used one relational operator in the previous example = (equal to). The full list is given in Table 5.1.

relational operator	meaning
=	equal to
>	greater than
<	less than
> = or = >	greater than or equal to
< = or = <	less than or equal to
< > or > <	not equal to

Table 5.1   Relational operators

The IF . . . THEN statement is useful for terminating the inputting of data, as it can be used to test for a final dummy value. This is a value which indicates the end of the data list, but which is not used in the calculations in the program. This is illustrated in Table 5.2, which shows a program to add numbers. The numbers are entered one at a time in response to the INPUT statement in line 30.

```
10 PRINT"ADD N NUMBERS"
11 PRINT
20 LET T=0
30 INPUT X
40 IF X<=0 THEN 70
50 LET T=T+X
60 GOTO 30
70 PRINT"TOTAL =";T
80 END
```

Table 5.2   Terminating with a dummy value

The program in Table 5.2 will stop when either a zero or a negative value is read into X. The IF . . . THEN statement must appear before the calculations involving X, so that the dummy value is not used in the calculations.

Another way to stop repetition of a set of instructions is to specify the number of times the loop has to be carried out, as shown in Table 5.3.

```
10 INPUT N
20 PRINT"ADD";N;"NUMBERS"
25 PRINT
30 LET I=0
35 LET T=0
40 INPUT X
50 LET T=T+X
60 LET I=I+1
70 IF I<N THEN 40
80 PRINT"TOTAL =";T
90 END
```

Table 5.3 Program to add N numbers

If line 30 in Table 5.3 read:

$$30 \text{ LET } I = 1$$

then line 70 would need to be:

$$70 \text{ IF } I < = N \text{ THEN } 40$$

This is because the value of I, after line 60 has been obeyed, is one greater than the number of numbers when the loop has been executed N times, if I is set to 1 to start with. This means the loop is terminated when $I = N + 1$.

5.3 Comparing character strings

The IF . . . THEN statement may also be used to compare character strings, since each character is represented by a unique combination of binary digits when stored in the computer. For example, if P\$ contains the character H, then:

$$25 \text{ IF } P\$ = \text{"H" THEN } 30$$

will be true and a branch will be made to line 30.

This facility is particularly useful for comparing names, addresses and similar information for business applications. You will need to refer to a list of codes used to represent characters in your computer's memory to find out which characters have a lower or higher value for greater than or less than tests (see Appendix C).

5.4   The FOR . . . NEXT statements

In section 5.2, the number of times a loop was executed was programmed by setting an initial value for the loop counter, testing for a final value, and incrementing the current value of the loop counter if the final value had not been reached. The FOR . . . NEXT statements have been designed to program these three operations in an easier way.

In the example to add N numbers, in Table 5.3, the variable I (used as the loop counter) was set to an initial value 0. 1 was added to I after the number had been read and added in, and finally a test was carried out (I < N) to determine whether the program should loop back or stop. FOR . . . NEXT statements will be used in an alternative version of the program. The FOR . . . NEXT statements consist of two lines of code. At the beginning of the loop the FOR statement is used to set up the initial conditions, the increment or STEP to be made at the end of the loop and the final value as follows:

line number FOR *variable* = *expression 1* TO *expression 2*
STEP *expression 3*

where expression 1 sets the initial value of the loop counter (also known as the index), expression 2 sets the final value of the loop counter, and expression 3 gives the increment to be added to the variable at the end of each pass through the set of instructions in the loop. If the STEP is equal to 1, both the word STEP and expression 3 may be omitted.

The final instruction in the loop has the format:

line number NEXT *variable*

where the variable has the same name as that given in the associated FOR statement.

The program in Table 5.3 can be amended as shown in

Table 5.4. A number will be read into X N times as controlled by the FOR . . . NEXT statements. I is set to 1 initially in line 35, then in line 60 I is incremented by 1 and if it is greater than N the program will go to line 80 and print the total, otherwise it goes back to line 40.

```
10 INPUT N
20 PRINT"ADD";N;"NUMBERS"
25 PRINT
30 LET T=0
35 FOR I=1 TO N
40 INPUT X
50 LET T=T+X
60 NEXT I
80 PRINT"TOTAL =";T
90 END
```

Table 5.4 Alternative program to add N numbers

Insert the instruction:

70 PRINT I

so that you can see the value of I after the loop has been executed for the required number of times.

You may use I within the loop, but you should avoid changing I (that is assigning a new value to I) within the loop as this changes the conditions set up by the FOR . . . NEXT statements. The problem flowcharted in Figure 5.1 may be coded as follows:

50 FOR I = 1 TO 21 STEP 2
60 PRINT I
70 NEXT I
80 END

The value of the increment given in the expression following STEP may be negative (so that the loop counter is decremented) or fractional. Table 5.5 shows a program

```
10 PRINT"START,END AND STEP"
15 PRINT"VARIABLES"
16 PRINT
20 INPUT A,B,C
30 FOR I=A TO B STEP C
40 PRINT I
50 NEXT I
60 END
```

Table 5.5   Start, end and step variables

where you can input the start, end and step as variables (A, B and C). Try a number of different combinations, including negative and fractional values, and see what happens. Table 5.6 shows a similar program where expressions have been used in place of simple variables.

```
10 PRINT"START,END AND STEP"
15 PRINT"EXPRESSIONS"
16 PRINT
20 INPUT A,B,C
30 FOR I=A+1 TO B/2 STEP C-3
40 PRINT I
50 NEXT I
60 END
```

Table 5.6   Start, end and step expressions

5.5   The ON . . . GOTO statement

The format of the ON . . . GOTO statement is

line number ON *expression*   GOTO *two or more line numbers separated by commas*

The integral part of the evaluated expression must be a positive number not greater than the *number* of line numbers after the GOTO part of the statement.

Control will pass to the first, second, third, etc. line

number after the GOTO if the integral part of the expression is equal to 1, 2, 3, etc.

For example, different calculations may need to be carried out according to a code, as in the following problem. A number of sets of data are to be input. Each set consists of a code (1, 2, 3, 4 or 5) and values of X and Y. Calculations are to be performed on each set of data according to the rules shown in Table 5.7.

Code	Calculation
1	$R = X + Y$
2	$R = X - Y$
3	$R = X*Y$
4	$R = X/Y$
5	$R = X \uparrow Y$

Table 5.7 Calculations for different codes

You can now write a program to tabulate the code, the X and Y values, and the results of the calculations.

Use the ON . . . GOTO statement to control which calculation is to be carried out according to its associated code. Draw a flowchart for the program, prepare test data, code and run your BASIC program. Remember the test data must test every branch in your program. You may input the codes and data in any order, that is the first set of data may have a code of, say, 3, the next a code of 1, etc. Compare your program with the one listed in Table A3. Suitable test data and calculated values are given in Appendix B.

5.6 Further use of the TAB function and FOR loops

The TAB function may be used with a variable or expression in the brackets following TAB, e.g. TAB(I), TAB(P − 1). The program given in Table 5.8 outputs a rectangle of variable dimensions, consisting of L1 dashes for the two lines across and L2 ↑s for the two vertical lines.

```
20 PRINT"START COLUMN POSITION"
30 INPUT P
40 PRINT"LENGTH ACROSS & DOWN"
50 INPUT L1,L2
60 LET K=1
70 PRINT TAB(P-1);
80 REM OUTPUT DASHES ACROSS
90 FOR I=1 TO L1
100 PRINT"-";
110 NEXT I
120 PRINT
130 IF K=2 THEN 240
140 REM OUTPUT "↑"S DOWN
150 FOR I=1 TO L2-2
160 PRINT TAB(P-1);"↑";
170 FOR J=1 TO L1-2
180 PRINT" ";
190 NEXT J
200 PRINT"↑"
210 NEXT I
220 LET K=K+1
230 GOTO 70
240 END
```

Table 5.8   Program to output a rectangle

Notes on Table 5.8

1   Lines 20 and 40 output a message to the user asking for data to be entered.

2   The PRINT statement in line 70 is terminated by a semi-colon (;); this will cause the *next* PRINT statement that is obeyed to output on to the *same* line.

3   Line 120 is necessary to cause the complete line of L1 dashes to be output. After passing through line 220, which sets K to 2, lines 90–120 are repeated to complete the rectangle and execution of the program is then terminated.

4   Lines 150–210 comprise a FOR loop which has another FOR loop (lines 170–190) wholly within it.

The FOR loops are said to be *nested* and this will be discussed further in Chapter 8. For each pass through the outer FOR loop, the inner loop is executed $L1-2$ times, so that a ↑ is output followed by some spaces and then another ↑. When line 190 is reached another pass through the outer loop is executed until $L2-2$ lines, consisting of ↑ spaces ↑, have been output.

In this case, the use of nested FOR loops could be avoided by replacing lines 160–200 by the following statement:

160 PRINT TAB(P − 1); "↑"; TAB(L1 − 1 + P); "↑"

Figure 5.2 Rectangle output from program

Figure 5.2 shows a rectangle output by the program when the following data was used:

$$7$$
$$20, 10$$

i.e. twenty dashes were output for the two lines across and eight ↑s for the two vertical lines.

You should enter the program given in Table 5.8 into your VIC and run it with different input data. Write another program to output a rectangle of variable width and depth in the centre of the screen, using graphics characters for the four corners and four sides. The program is listed in Table A4.

5.7   Problems

The following problems all refer to the name and address program given in Table 2.1, p. 15.

Problem 1 – Print options

Amend the program in Table 2.1 to allow selection of any combination of the three print options:

code	option
H	Letter heading
N	Notebook label
L	Envelope label
F	Stop execution of program

The amendments are given in Table A5.

Problem 2 – Letter headings

Amend the program in Table 2.1 to enable the letter heading print position and the number of headed sheets required to be entered at run time. The amendments are given in Table A6.

Problem 3 – Notebook labels

Amend the program in Table 2.1 so that the name in N\$ is output centrally in a complete border of asterisks. Allow for the number of labels required, the length of the name, and the number of labels to be output per page to be entered at run time. The amendments are given in Table A7.

Problem 4 – Envelope labels

Amend the program in Table 2.1 to enable the total number of labels required and the number of labels per page to be entered at run time. The amendments are given in Table A8.

Note: Loops will need to be inserted into the program for problems 2, 3 and 4 to cause the required number of letter headings, notebook and envelope labels to be printed.

6 POKE, PEEK and Colour

6.1 Character codes

As explained in Chapter 1 characters and numbers are stored in a computer as binary patterns. Standard binary codes have been established by different organisations. The American Standard Code for Information Interchange (ASCII) has been widely adopted and Appendix C gives these codes as implemented on the VIC. Characters can be converted into these codes and *vice versa* by the use of ASC and CHR$ string functions. These and further string functions are described below.

6.1.1 *CHR$*

This function returns the character corresponding to a specified ASCII code, i.e.

$$10 \text{ LET A\$} = \text{CHR\$}(66)$$

The ASCII code for the letter B is 66, so the above statement stores B in A$. Words can be built up by concatenation, i.e.

$$10 \text{ LET A\$} = \text{CHR\$}(66) + \text{CHR\$}(69)$$

results in A$ = BE, where 69 is the ASCII code for E.

Note that as CHR$ returns the ASCII code, variables can be set if required to various control characters (i.e. Return).

6.1.2 *ASC*

This function is the opposite of CHR$ in that it returns the ASCII code number for a specified character, i.e.

$$10 \text{ LET X} = \text{ASC(“E”)}$$

results in X = 69.

If the argument is a string variable the ASCII code of the first character is returned, i.e.

$$5 \text{ LET T\$} = \text{“TOTAL”}$$
$$10 \text{ LET X} = \text{ASC(T\$)}$$

results in X = 84.

6.1.3 *LEN*

This function returns the length of a string. For example, changing line 10 to:

$$10 \text{ LET L} = \text{LEN(T\$)}$$

would set L = 5.

6.1.4 *LEFT\$, RIGHT\$*

These functions return the leftmost or rightmost specified number of characters from a string, e.g.

$$10 \text{ LET B\$} = \text{LEFT\$(T\$,2)}$$

returns the leftmost two characters from the string T\$, i.e.
B\$ = TO, similarly,

$$10 \text{ LET E\$} = \text{RIGHT\$(T\$,3)}$$

leaves E\$ = TAL

6.1.5 *MID\$*

This function returns a substring of n characters starting with the ith character, i.e.

$$10 \text{ LET C\$} = \text{MID\$(T\$,2,3)}$$

results in C\$ = OTA where n = 3 and i = 2.

6.1.6   *STR$*

This function converts a numeric argument to the string equivalent of its PRINTed form, i.e.

$$10 \text{ LET N} = 20$$
$$20 \text{ LET X\$} = \text{STR\$(N)}$$

results in X$ containing "20" as a string, thus

$$30 \text{ LET Y\$} = \text{"VIC"} + \text{X\$}$$
$$40 \text{ PRINT Y\$}$$

results in,

VIC 20

being printed. Note that the string version of the numeric contains a leading blank (the suppressed + sign).

6.1.7   *VAL*

This function is the opposite of STR$. The string is examined, left to right and the *first* recognisable number format is returned, i.e.

X = VAL("VIC 20") results in X = 20
X = VAL("−78.97.65") results in X = −78.97

6.2   POKE and PEEK

The POKE command allows you to place any specified value directly into a required memory location. Its general form is, POKE x,y where the value of x specifies the memory location and y the value to be POKEd, i.e.

POKE 36879,93

The above command places the value 93 into memory location 36879. In this case, location 36879 happens to be the one that determines the colour of the screen. The value 93 causes the screen to go completely green. A more detailed explanation of the control of colour is given in section 6.3.

The most common use for POKE on the VIC is to control the colour, sound and position of characters on the screen. Advanced programming techniques can involve PEEKing and POKEing to a special area of computer memory known as zero page, in order to achieve special effects that are not available from BASIC. Although PEEKing and POKEing cannot in any way damage your VIC, you should first master simple applications, such as POKEing VIC screen memory and the VIC control registers, before trying out more sophisticated techniques. If at any time the VIC 'crashes', e.g the cursor disappears etc. then pressing the STOP and RESTORE keys simultaneously will reset the VIC without the loss of your program.

The PEEK function allows access to the contents of a specified memory location. PEEK(x) returns the value of the contents of location x. The value returned can be assigned to be a variable in the usual way, i.e.

```
10 LET S = PEEK(36879)
20 PRINT S
```

Running the above program immediately after starting the VIC should result in S having the value 27.

PEEKing may be used in games and animation to determine the 'status' of parts of the screen, i.e. whether a missile is now occupying the target's location, thereby implying a hit.

Variables can be used with both PEEK and POKE so that all the following are examples of valid syntax:

```
POKE X,Z
POKE X + L*22, Z
PEEK (X + L*22)
IF A$ = CHR$(PEEK(K)) THEN Y
```

6.3 The VIC colour system

The VIC colour system allows independent control of the colour of the screen, its border and any individual character.

The border can be set to any one of eight colours and the screen to any one of sixteen colours. They are set via a single POKE command to location 36879; the value being POKEd determines the border-screen colour combination. Appendix D gives the required value for all combinations. For example, the combination at start-up is a cyan border and white screen which can be subsequently restored by:

POKE 36879,27

The program in Table 6.1 demonstrates all the screen and border combinations. Note that when the screen is the same colour as the characters, the characters are not readable and apparently disappear. The program consists of two loops; the outer loop (lines 10–60) sets S to successive screen values associated with a black border and hence to the first entry in each row of Appendix D. The inner loop (lines 20–50) determines the column position and hence S + B represents the value to be POKEd. Line 40 is a delay loop to allow each colour combination to be viewed.

```
10 FOR S=8 TO 248 STEP 16
20 FOR B=0 TO 7
30 POKE 36879,S+B
40 FOR D=1 TO 1000:NEXT D
50 NEXT B
60 NEXT S
70 END
```

Table 6.1 Demonstration of border and screen colours

Control over the colour of the characters can be achieved in several ways and is discussed next.

6.4 Colour control of characters

The colour of characters can be programmed by the use of specific keys, by setting variables to specific character codes or by POKEing direct to the screen.

The colour of characters output to the screen from the current position of the cursor onwards can be set by keying CTRL simultaneously with one of the labelled colour keys. This keying sequence can also be incorporated within quotes in a PRINT statement, i.e.

10 PRINT *"CTRL and Red key* THIS PRINTS RED"

Alternatively, the keying of CTRL and a colour can be assigned to a string variable which is then incorporated in a PRINT statement, i.e.

10 C\$ = *"CTRL and Red key"*
20 PRINT C\$;"THIS PRINTS RED"

A third way of PRINTing in a specified colour is to use the appropriate character code as found in Appendix C. The program in Table 6.2 illustrates this method where the character codes are read from a series of DATA statements. This method of changing the colour of characters is useful for printing headings.

```
10 FOR L=1 TO 8
20 READ C,C$
30 PRINT CHR$(C);"THIS IS ";C$
40 NEXT L
100 DATA 144,BLACK
110 DATA 5,WHITE
120 DATA 28,RED
130 DATA 159,CYAN
140 DATA 156,PURPLE
150 DATA 30,GREEN
160 DATA 31,BLUE
170 DATA 158,YELLOW
180 END
```

Table 6.2 Printing strings in different colours

The space bar can be used to produce 'bars' of colour by use of the RVS ON and RVS OFF keys. If the reverse character set is turned on by the RVS ON key a space becomes a solid block of whatever colour is in operation. This is also programmable, i.e.

10 PRINT "*CTRL and RVS ON key CTRL and Red key* ▽▽▽▽▽"

produces a red bar five spaces long. Note that RVS ON and RVS OFF both have character codes (18 and 146, respectively) that can be used in programs in the same way as the codes for colours. Thus the previous example instead could be:

10 PRINT CHR$(18);CHR$(28);"▽▽▽▽▽"

The fourth method of producing coloured characters is to use the POKE command and is discussed in the next section.

6.5 POKEing coloured characters

The screen of the VIC is memory mapped, that is each possible character position on the screen has an associated memory location. For example, the top left hand corner position corresponds to memory location 7680 on the basic VIC and by POKEing this address with a particular value the appropriate character will appear on the screen in white (for this to be visible the screen colour should be set, for the time being, to another colour). The screen codes for each key are given in Appendix E. Note that these codes do not correspond to the character codes of Appendix C, and are only relevant for POKEing to the screen. Thus,

POKE 7680,83

will produce a white heart in the 'home position'. By adding 128 to the code its equivalent reverse character is obtained.

For each screen memory location there is a corresponding colour code memory location, e.g. 38400 is the colour location corresponding to the screen position 7680. It is important to ensure that the correct *matching* colour location is used with the required screen memory location. The colour of the character POKEd to a location can be controlled by POKEing a value *one less* than the number shown on the colour keys, e.g. 2 for red. Thus,

POKE 7680,83 : POKE 38400,2

will produce a red heart in the 'home position'.

The screen memory locations together with their associated colour locations are given in Appendix F. These locations change if the VIC is expanded beyond an additional 3K. For this reason it is advisable, when writing programs that PEEK and POKE to the screen, to use expressions that relate to the 'home position' and the required offset. This expression can also use the required row and column numbers to calculate the memory location, i.e.

100 SM = 7680 : CM = 38400
110 POKE SM + 22*R + C, 83
120 POKE CM + 22*R + C, 2

If you are using a VIC system with more than 3K of additional RAM expansion, you will need to set SM to 4096 and CM to 37888.

The routine above will POKE a red heart to row R, column C. If the screen memory and colour locations change only line 100 need be adjusted.

Table 6.3 gives a simple program illustrating the use of POKE. This program POKEs a series of different coloured hearts near the centre of the screen. The starting position is row 11 (line 110). A loop (lines 120–150) prints a different coloured heart in turn in columns C + I (columns 6 to 13 inclusive). The loop counter, I, is also used to determine the colour, I−1 in line 140.

```
90 PRINT"⊐":REM CLEAR
100 SM=7680:CM=38400
110 R=11:C=6
120 FOR I=1 TO 8
130 POKE SM+22*R+C+I,83
140 POKE CM+22*R+C+I,I-1
150 NEXT I
160 END
```

Table 6.3 POKEing coloured hearts to screen

6.6 Histogram example

The program in Table 6.4 illustrates the use of colours to produce a histogram. This routine plots ten vertical lines, in red, over a scale from 0 to 10.

```
10 PRINT"⊐":REM CLEAR
20 PRINT"******HISTOGRAM******"
25 PRINT
30 FOR L=10 TO 1 STEP-1
40 L$="   "+STR$(L)
50 PRINT RIGHT$(L$,4);" ⊐"
60 NEXT L
70 PRINT"   0 ⊓⊓⊓⊓⊓⊓⊓⊓⊓⊓"
80 FOR P= 1 TO 10
90 READ D
100 IF D=0 THEN 150
110 FOR H=1 TO D
120 POKE 7971-(H*22)+P,160
130 POKE 38691-(H*22)+P,2
140 NEXT H
150 NEXT P
160 DATA 5,7,8,3,5,2,6,0,1,6
170 END
```

Table 6.4 Histogram routine

Line 10 clears the screen and line 20 prints the main heading. Lines 30 to 60 form a loop that produces the vertical scale. The string handling in these lines causes the numbers, obtained from the loop count, to be aligned correctly. The graphics character in line 50 forms part of the scaled vertical axis. Line 70 produces the horizontal axis.

In this example, data is contained in a DATA line (160) and is read as required for each column in line 90 into the variable D. The histogram is built up by POKEing red reverse characters vertically over ten columns as required. Lines 80 to 150 form an outer loop that repeats the inner loop for each column. If the histogram has zero entry then line 100 causes the inner loop to be bypassed.

The inner loop (lines 110–140) POKEs a reverse character space (32 + 128 = 160) vertically D times.

6.7 Animation

The building up of the bars in the histogram example represents a simple form of animation. However, more elaborate animation such as that used in games requires characters to move up, down and across the screen. The illusion of movement is obtained by POKEing the character into a suitable adjacent screen location and then POKEing a space into the preceding position.

```
5 PRINT"□":REM CLEAR
10 SM=7680:CM=38400
20 S=SM+22*8
30 C=CM+22*8
40 FOR I=0 TO 21
50 POKE S+I,42
60 POKE C+I,2
70 POKE S+I-1,32
80 FOR D=1 TO 100:NEXT D
90 NEXT I
100 POKE S+21,32
110 END
```

Table 6.5   An example of simple animation

A simple example of this is given by the program in Table 6.5. This program causes an asterisk to move across the screen from left to right in row 8 (note that the top row is row zero). Lines 10 to 30 set the initial screen and colour locations to the first position of row 8. The loop (lines 40–90) moves the required character to each column along that row and colour it red (line 60). Line 70 within the loop puts a space into the preceding column. A delay loop in line 80 stops the asterisk moving too fast. Line 100 puts a space into the final position of the asterisk on exiting the loop.

6.8   Problem

Use graphics characters to build up a simple picture of a face on the screen. Introduce animation that causes the face to alternately sulk and smile.

An example of such a routine is given in Table A9.

7   Other Functions

7.1   Mathematical functions

Commonly used routines, such as those required for obtaining the integral part of a number (INT), the logarithm and antilogarithm of a number (LOG and EXP), and trigonometric functions (e.g. SIN) are available as library functions in BASIC. Examples of a variety of these functions will be given in the following sections.

Further background on mathematical functions and problems involving these are given in *The Pocket Calculator* L. R. Carter and E. Huzan, Teach Yourself Books, 1979.

7.2   Arguments

Each function name is followed by an expression (the argument) in brackets. The function operates on the argument, that is, the value of the expression is used in the standard routine represented by the function name. For example:

$$100 \text{ LET } S = SQR(B*B - 4*A*C)$$

will evaluate the square root of the expression in brackets, i.e $B^2 - 4AC$, and put the result in cell S.

There may be restrictions regarding the values of the argument associated with a function. For example, it is not possible to take the square root of a negative number, therefore the argument used with SQR must not have a negative value. The TAB function followed by a semicolon causes characters to be output in the column following the argument value; therefore, this value must correspond to a possible column position. A comma in place of the semi-colon will have a different effect.

7.3   Using library functions

Library functions are used in LET or PRINT statements on their own or in expressions of any complexity. These expressions may contain further library functions. The evaluation is, as usual, working from the innermost brackets outwards.

7.4   Truncation

You have already used the library function INT to obtain the integral part of a number which has decimal places. The INT function gives the largest integer which is not greater than the argument. Therefore, if the argument is a *positive* number, the decimal places are dropped and the number is said to be truncated after INT has been used. For example:

$$110 \text{ LET B} = \text{INT(A)}$$

puts 15 into B if A is 15.36. Remember A will remain unchanged after the LET statement has been obeyed, so it will still contain 15.36.

However, if A contains −15.36 then the integer placed into B is *not* −15 (since this is larger than −15.36) *but* −16; in this case, B does not contain the truncated value of A.

To obtain the truncated value of a *negative* number, the sign must be removed from the number before the INT function is applied, using the function ABS which takes the absolute value of its argument (i.e. the sign is ignored), and the function SGN used. SGN gives the value of 1 if its argument has a positive value, −1 if its argument has a negative value, and a zero if the value of its argument is zero. For example:

$$120 \text{ LET B} = \text{SGN(A)} * \text{INT(ABS(A))}$$

multiplies the integral part of the absolute value of A by its sign, so that B will contain the truncated value of A when A is positive or negative. Assuming A contains −15.36, as in the previous example, then ABS(A) gives 15.36, INT(ABS(A)) gives 15, and SGN(A)*INT(ABS(A)) multiplies 15 by −1 giving −15.

7.5 Rounding

Numbers often need to be rounded to a nearest number of decimal places or to a nearest value in general. Adding 0.5 to a number before truncating it will cause the number to be rounded to the nearest integer (whole number). For example:

$$130 \text{ LET B} = \text{INT}(A + 0.5)$$

puts 24 in B if A contains, say 24.3, and 25 in B if A contains, say 24.5 or 24.6. The program shown in Table 7.1 illustrates this method of rounding; angles input in decimals of a degree are output in degrees and minutes, rounded to the nearest minute.

```
20 PRINT" ANGLE    DEGS    MINS"
30 PRINT
40 INPUT A
50 IF A=0 THEN 110
60 LET D=INT(A)
70 REM ROUND
80 LET M=INT((A-D)*60+0.5)
90 PRINT A;TAB(10);D;TAB(17);M
100 GOTO 40
110 END
```

Table 7.1 Rounding to nearest minute

To round a number to a certain number of decimal places, you need to divide the number by a scaling factor before adding 0.5, truncating, and finally multiplying by the scaling factor. For example, to round to three decimal places the scaling factor is 0.001:

$$140 \text{ LET P2} = \text{INT(P1/0.001} + 0.5)*0.001$$

puts 3.142 into P2 when P1 contains 3.14159.

In general, if the scaling factor is contained in F then an expression may be rounded by using:

$$\text{INT((expression)/F} + 0.5)*F$$

This will work also if, for example, you wish to round a number to the nearest 10; in this case, F = 10.

7.6 Square roots

The library function for obtaining a square root is SQR. Remember the argument must not have a negative value. You can use SGN to test the sign, as shown in Table 7.2.

```
70 INPUT N
80 FOR I=1 TO N
90 INPUT A,B,C:PRINT
100 LET R=B*B-4*A*C
110 IF SGN(R)=-1 THEN 150
120 LET R=SQR(R)
130 PRINT"SQUARE ROOT ="
135 PRINTR;"FOR";A;B;C
140 GOTO 160
150 PRINT"RESULT NEGATIVE"
155 PRINT"FOR";A;B;C:PRINT
160 NEXT I
170 END
```

Table 7.2 Use of SGN and SQR

The program given in Table 7.3 calculates and outputs the diameter in metres (rounded to two decimal places) of cylindrical tanks, given the volume V (in litres of water) and three standard heights in metres. The formula for the volume of a cylinder of height h, and radius r is:

$$V = \pi r^2 h$$

Therefore, the diameter d is given by:

$$d = 2r = 2\sqrt{\frac{V}{\pi h}}$$

```
20 PRINT"VOLUME HEIGHT DIAMETER"
30 PRINT"LTRS.    M.       M."
40 PRINT"------ ------ --------"
50 DATA 1,1.25,1.75
60 INPUT V
80 IF V=0 THEN 160
85 PRINT
90 FOR I=1 TO 3
100 READ H
110 LET D=INT(SQR(V/(1000*3.142*H))*200+0.5)/100
120 PRINT TAB(1);V;TAB(8);H;TAB(16);D
130 NEXT I
140 RESTORE
150 GOTO 60
160 END
```

Table 7.3 Calculation of diameter of cylindrical tanks

In the problem, the three standard heights are given in a DATA statement. For each volume V the diameter D is calculated and output using each of the three standard heights in turn. Every time the READ H statement (line 100) is obeyed, the next value in the DATA statement is taken. That is, the first time through the FOR loop H is taken to be 1, the second time 1.25, and the third time 1.75. The DATA pointer then needs to be reset to the beginning of the DATA values ready for a further three passes through the FOR loop with the next value of V. This is achieved by the RESTORE statement in line 140. Use the program to find the diameter of tanks which have volumes of 500 and 1000 litres (1000 litres = 1 m³). The answers are shown in Table 7.4

VOLUME LTRS.	HEIGHT M.	DIAMETER M.
500	1	.8
500	1.25	.71
500	1.75	.6
1000	1	1.13
1000	1.25	1.01
1000	1.75	.85

Table 7.4   Output from program given in Table 7.3

7.7   Trigonometric functions

The sine, cosine and tangent of angles are obtained by using the function names SIN, COS and TAN respectively, followed by the angle in brackets (expressed in radians). For example:

$$100 \text{ LET X} = \text{COS(B)}$$

will put the cosine of B (radians) in cell X.

Only the inverse tangent (arctangent) is available as the function ATN. This has as the argument the tangent of the required angle. The angle obtained will be in radians $-\pi/2$ to $\pi/2$.

For angle x, $\tan x = \dfrac{\sin x}{\cos x}$ and $\sin^2 x + \cos^2 x = 1$.

Therefore, the inverse sine and inverse cosine of x may be expressed as follows:

$$\sin^{-1} x = \tan^{-1} \left[\frac{\sin x}{\sqrt{(1 - \sin^2 x)}} \right] \qquad \ldots (7.1)$$

$$\cos^{-1} x = -\tan^{-1} \left[\frac{\cos x}{\sqrt{(1 - \cos^2 x)}} \right] \qquad \ldots (7.2)$$

When $0 < x < \pi/2$ cosines are positive $= \cos x$
When $\pi/2 < x < \pi$ cosines are negative $= -\cos(\pi - x)$

Equation (7.2) is true for both cases. When $\cos x > 0$, the expression in brackets is positive and equation (7.2) gives the required angle as x. When $\cos x < 0$, the expression in brackets is negative and equation (7.2) gives the required angle as $\pi - x$.

The following BASIC statements may be used to find angle A in radians given that the sine of the angle is S or the cosine of the angle is C:

        110 LET A = ATN(S/SQR(1 − S∗S))
        120 LET A = − ATN(C/SQR(1 − C∗C)) + 1.5708

where $\pi/2 \simeq 1.5708$
Note: You must avoid using the above formulae when S = 1 (required angle is $\pi/2$) or C = 1 (required angle is 0).

π is available as a library function with your VIC. Alternatively, its numeric value may be used as a constant, or ATN(1)∗4 will calculate π, since the tan of $\pi/4$ radians is 1.

7.8   Logarithms and antilogarithms

The logarithms and antilogarithms of expressions are given by the functions LOG and EXP, respectively. For example, the xth root of a number may be found by dividing the log of the number (y) by x and taking the antilog; this may be expressed as shown in the following BASIC statement:

$$100 \text{ LET R} = \text{EXP(LOG(Y)/X)}$$

After this statement has been obeyed, R will contain the required root.

The function LOG gives the logarithm of its argument to base e; these are known as Naperian (or natural) logarithms. Since,

$$\log_{10} y = \frac{\log_e y}{\log_e 10}$$

the following BASIC statement finds the log of a number (Y) to base 10:

$$110 \text{ LET T} = \text{LOG(Y)/LOG(10)}$$

Similarly, the antilog is found by multiplying the log to base 10 by $\log_e 10$ and taking the antilog of the result as follows:

$$120 \text{ LET A} = \text{EXP(T*LOG(10))}$$

e has the value 2.7182818 to 8 significant figures. The function EXP raises e to the Xth power, where X is its argument. That is, $\text{EXP(X)} = e^x$; the use of EXP is illustrated further in the next section.

7.9   Hyperbolic functions

Hyperbolic functions may be expressed in terms of e^x. For example:

$$\sinh x = \frac{1}{2} (e^x - e^{-x})$$

$$\cosh h = \frac{1}{2} (e^x + e^{-x})$$

$$\tanh x = \frac{\sinh x}{\cosh x} = \frac{e^x - e^{-x}}{e^x + e^{-x}}$$

The sinh of the number held in cell X will be placed into cell Y by the following LET statement:

$$110 \text{ LET Y} = (\text{EXP(X)} - \text{EXP(}-\text{X)})/2$$

7.10   TAB function

The TAB function has already been used in several examples. The definition of TAB is summarised below. The TAB function may only be used in PRINT statements to give the next output column position.

If TAB(P) is followed by a semicolon, then the variable or expression following the semicolon will be output starting at column INT(P+1). P may be any expression whose value lies between 0 and 255.

7.11 Random numbers

Pseudo random numbers may be obtained by the use of the function RND. This function chooses a number at random between 0 and 1. This facility can be used in programs to form the basis of chance outcome in games, and to simulate randomness in scientific and business applications.

The function is RND(X), where X is a dummy number having any value. The value of X determines the starting point of the string of numbers generated, that is, RND(7) will generate a difference sequence from RND(3). However, because RND(7), for example, is fixed within a program the same sequence will be generated each time the program is run.

The random numbers generated will usually need to be manipulated. For example, to represent the throw of a die integer values between 1 and 6 need to be randomly generated. This may be done with the following instruction:

$$100 \text{ LET T} = \text{INT}(6*\text{RND}(3) + 1)$$

The +1 is required as otherwise the truncated integer would lie between 0 and 5.

When it is required to generate numbers to represent a sample from a uniform distribution a single statement similar to the above will be sufficient. In more advanced cases of simulation, it is often required to sample from a given frequency distribution. A subroutine suitable for these circumstances is described in Chapter 9.

7.12 User defined functions

You may define your own functions by using a DEF FNx statement, which has the following format:

line number DEF FN*x*(*variable*) = *expression*

Each user-defined function must have a unique name within the program as given by FN*x*, where *x* is a variable name.

Each function has a dummy argument given by the variable in brackets above. The actual argument used when the function is subsequently referenced in the program will be different from the dummy argument in the function definition. For example, the previous expression used to round a number can now be defined as a function as follows:

$$50 \text{ DEF FNR}(A) = \text{INT}(A/F + 0.5)*F$$

This can be used subsequently in the same program to round a number to, say, the nearest 100 and to one decimal place as shown in Table 7.5.

```
50 DEF FNR(A)=INT(A/F+0.5)*F
60 READ B,C
70 DATA 650,32.55,649,32.54,651,32.56,0,0
80 IF B = 0 THEN 190
100 REM ROUND B TO NEAREST 100
110 LET F=100
120 LET B1=FNR(B)
130 REM ROUND C TO 1 DECIMAL PLACE
140 LET F=0.1
150 LET C1=FNR(C)
160 PRINT "B =";B;"B1 =";B1,"C =";C;"C1 =";C1
170 PRINT
180 GOTO 60
190 END
```

Table 7.5 Program to round numbers

A user-defined function may contain another user-defined function in its definition. For example, the program given in Table 7.6 tabulates the sines of a number of angles (given) and the corresponding angles expressed in degrees to two decimal places.

```
20 PRINT"  SINE    DEGREES"
30 PRINT"  ————    ————"
40 PRINT
50 DEF FNR(A)=INT(A/0.1+0.5)*0.1
60 DEF FND(U)=180/(ATN(1)*4)
70 DEF FNA(S)=(ATN(S/SQR(1-S*S)))*FND(U)
80 INPUT X
90 IF X=0 THEN 160
100 IF X<>1 THEN 130
110 LET D=90
120 GOTO 140
130 LET D=FNR(FNA(X))
140 PRINT TAB(1);X;TAB(9);D
150 GOTO 80
160 END
```

Table 7.6 Sines and angles (in degrees)

7.13 Problems

Problem 1 – Radius of circumcircle

Write a program to find the radius of a circular track passing through points which form a triangle. The radius (r) of the circumcircle of a triangle is given by:

$$r = \frac{a}{2\sin A} = \frac{b}{2\sin B} = \frac{c}{2\sin C}$$

where a, b, c and A, B, C are the sides and angles of the triangle.

The program is listed in Table A10, and the answer for a = 452 metres, b = 386 metres and c = 739 metres is given in Appendix B. (*Note:* cos B = $(a^2 + c^2 - b^2)/2ac$.)

Problem 2 – Areas of triangles

The area of a triangle, with sides a, b and c and angles A, B and C, may be calculated if the three sides *or* two sides and the included angle are given, by using one of the following formulae:

area of triangle = $\sqrt{(s(s-a)(s-b)(s-c))}$
where $2s = a + b + c$

or   area = ½absin C or ½bcsin A or ½acsin B

Write a program to tabulate the areas of the triangles given in Table 7.7, using suitable headings. Note *unknown* values have been set to zero. Output all areas in square cm to one decimal place. The program is listed in Table A11, and the answers are given in Appendix B.

| | Sides of triangle (cm) | | | Included angle |
	a	b	c	(degrees)
	17.2	9.8	14.1	0
	0	74	98	125.4
	292	0	405	30.5
	10.3	15.6	0	69
dummy values	−1	0	0	0

Table 7.7   Data used to calculate areas of triangles

Problem 3 – Volumes of solids

The volume of a solid of uniform cross-sectional area (A) and height (H) is given by:

$$V = A \times H$$

The uniform cross-sectional areas of some common solids are given in Table 7.8 together with their codes.

Write a program to calculate the volumes of the solids given in Table 7.8. All dimensions are in cm. The name of the solid is to be held in a DATA statement. Output the name of the solid and its volume. Code 0 can be used to terminate execution of the program. Suitable test data is given in Table 7.9, but include some extra data of your own.

Code	Solid	Cross-sectional area
1	cuboid	L × W
2	cylinder	$\pi \times R^2$
3	hexagonal bar	$\frac{1}{2}\sqrt{27} \times D^2$

L = length   W = width   R = radius   D = length of side

Table 7.8   Some solids with uniform cross-sectional areas

Code	1st dimension (L or R or D)	2nd dimension (W or zero)	Height (H)	Required no. of decimal places
2	4.5	0	1.75	2
3	12.6	0	250	0
1	5.3	7.0	4.2	1

Table 7.9   Data for 'Volumes of solids' problem

The program is listed in Table A12, and the answers are given in Appendix B. The program presented in Table A12 allows the user to round the answer using a scaling factor (F) to give the required number of decimal places (see section 7.5).

8 Arrays

8.1 Lists and tables

So far single memory cells have been referenced by single variable names.

Many problems involve processing a number of variables in exactly the same way. In these programs, it is much more convenient to use the same name to reference a number of memory cells whose contents are processed by the same set of instructions in the program; a subscript is used in association with the variable name to identify uniquely each particular memory cell. For example, the program given in

```
10 INPUT N
20 FOR I=1 TO N
30 INPUT A(I)
40 NEXT I
50 PRINT"NUMBERS > 10"
60 PRINT
70 FOR I=1 TO N
80 IF A(I) <= 10 THEN 100
90 PRINT A(I)
100 NEXT I
110 PRINT
120 PRINT
130 PRINT"NEGATIVE NUMBERS"
135 PRINT
140 FOR I=1 TO N
150 IF A(I) >=0 THEN 170
160 PRINT A(I)
170 NEXT I
180 PRINT
190 END
```

Table 8.1   Program to output numbers >10 and negative numbers

Table 8.1 inputs a list of N numbers and outputs a list of numbers that are greater than 10, and a list of numbers that are negative, using two passes through the stored data.

If N is equal to 9, then the list of 9 numbers is input into memory cells $A(1)$, $A(2)$, . . ., $A(9)$, since in the FOR loop (lines 20–40) I takes the values 1–9. I is the subscript and A is the name of an array of nine elements. Each element of the array may be referenced by the array name and the subscript referring to its position in the array. That is, $A(4)$ refers to the fourth number input into the array A, which is the memory cell between those occupied by $A(3)$ and $A(5)$.

Your BASIC system starts numbering the elements of an array at 0, that is, the first element of the array is referenced by $A(0)$. The program given in Table 8.1 may be amended so that it can be used to input and process nine numbers starting at $A(0)$ by changing the initial value of I to 0 in each FOR statement, lines 20, 70 and 140. N would need to be input as 8 instead of 9 in this case.

Try running the program given in Table 8.1 with the following nine numbers:

$$6, 12, -30, 10, -4, 47, 9, 0, 58$$

The output for this data is shown in Table 8.2.

NUMBERS > 10
    12
    47
    58

NEGATIVE NUMBERS
    −30
    −4

Table 8.2   Output from program given in Table 8.1

Array A, in the previous example, is called a one-dimensional array because it has one subscript. A one-dimensional array is a list, and a two-dimensional array is a table. A three-dimensional array is more difficult to visualise; an example would be to have the page number of a book as the third dimension (subscript), and the lines and columns on a page forming a table referenced by the other two subscripts. The subscripts are separated by commas within the brackets following the name of the array, so that T$(3,2,8) could refer to the third line and second column on the eighth page of a book.

8.2   Naming arrays

Arrays used for holding numbers must be called by a variable name followed by the subscripts in brackets.

Array names which are identical to single variable names may be used in the same program. That is, the BASIC system will distinguish between A used as a single variable and A (subscript(s)) used as an array element for storing numbers, and A$ used as a single string variable and A$ (subscript(s)) used for storing character strings.

8.3   Subscripts

The subscripts that may be used with array names may consist of any expression. However, since the subscripts refer to unique positions in the array which is stored in memory cells in the computer, the individual subscripts must have positive values which the system will truncate to integer values (zero is a possible value for a subscript as explained previously).

The integer values of the subscripts must lie within the bounds of the array. For example, in the program given in Table 8.1 the BASIC system automatically allocates eleven memory cells (subscripts 0–10) in the absence of a DIM statement, which will be explained in the next section. If N were input as, say, 20 then elements referenced in the FOR statement beyond the A(10) element would be outside the defined storage of the array (i.e. outside the bounds of the array); in this case an execution error would occur.

8.4 The DIM statement

The DIM statement is used to define storage for arrays which have subscripts whose values are greater than ten. Although the DIM statements can appear anywhere in the program (before the array is accessed) it is better to place it at the beginning of the program so that it is separate from the main logic.

The format of the DIM statement is:

line number DIM list of array variables separated by commas

The array variables in the list may be ordinary or string variables; each variable name is followed by subscripts, separated by commas, in brackets.

For example, array X is to be used to store a list of up to fifty numbers, and array T\$ is to be used to hold a table comprising a maximum of 5 rows and 7 columns.

The DIM statement to define storage for these two arrays is:

$$30 \text{ DIM } X(50), T\$(5,7)$$

X will have fifty-one memory cells of storage reserved referenced by $X(0), X(1), X(2), \ldots, X(50)$. T\$ will have a total of forty-eight cells reserved, the first cell being referenced by $T\$(0,0)$ and the last cell by $T\$(5,7)$.

Notice that storage is reserved for the *maximum* array size in each case. A particular run of your program may require less storage than the maximum; this is acceptable or alternatively you can input values for the variable subscripts in the DIM statement before it is used (this is known as dynamic dimensioning). Note that the dimensioning may only be done *once* during the program run. For example, the DIM statement below requires K, L and M to be input at run time.

$$40 \text{ DIM } X(K), T\$(L,M)$$

More than one DIM statement may be used in a program, but the *same* array name may *not* appear in more than one DIM statement in a program. For example:

$$\left.\begin{array}{l} 50 \text{ DIM } B\$(30,8),A\$(60),A(20,20) \\ 60 \text{ DIM } D(100),C\$(5,7,6) \end{array}\right\} \text{correct}$$

is correct.

$$\left.\begin{array}{l} 70 \text{ DIM } B\$(30,8),A\$(60),A(20,20) \\ 80 \text{ DIM } D(100),A(20,20),C\$(5,7,6) \end{array}\right\} \text{incorrect}$$

will produce an error because A(20,20) appears in the DIM statements in line 70 *and* in line 80.

It is important to note that the DIM statement may be used to override the automatic storage allocation for small arrays. For example, if array A is to contain a maximum of six cells and array B a maximum of four cells, then DIM A(5),B(3) will cause the *exact* storage required to be allocated, thus *saving* storage compared with the automatic allocation of eleven cells for each array.

8.5   Nested FOR loops

A FOR loop may lie wholly within another FOR loop, as was shown in Table 5.8, Chapter 5. This facility is particu-

1	2	3	4
5	6	7	8
9	10	11	12

Table 8.3   Input data for 'Nested FOR loops' program

1	5	9
2	6	10
3	7	11
4	8	12

Table 8.4 Table to be output

larly useful for manipulating arrays. For example, the data given in Table 8.3 is to be input into a two-dimensional array called A and output in the form shown in Table 8.4. The program given in Table 8.5 uses nested FOR loops to achieve this; try running this program.

```
10 DIM A(3,4)
20 DATA 1,2,3,4,5,6,7,8,9,10,11,12
30 FOR I=1 TO 3
40 FOR J=1 TO 4
50 READ A(I,J)
60 NEXT J
70 NEXT I
80 FOR I=1 TO 4
90 FOR J=1 TO 3
100 PRINT A(J,I);
110 NEXT J
120 PRINT
130 NEXT I
140 END
```

Table 8.5 Program using nested FOR loops

8.6 Problems

Write programs for the following problems.

Problem 1 – Copying an array

Copy an array A comprising N elements into an array B, of the same size as A, in reverse order. For example, if N is 20,

A(20) will go into B(1), A(19) into B(2), etc. Assume N is always a multiple of 5, and output array B in rows of 5 columns.

The program is listed in Table A13.

Problem 2 – Sum of elements

Sum the elements on the diagonals of an M × M array. Allow for M to be odd (as well as even) when the central element must be added in only *once*. Test your program in one run with an odd *and* an even value of M. Output the array and the sum of the elements on the diagonals in each case.

The program is listed in Table A14.

Problem 3 – Sorting a list of numbers

Sort a list of N numbers, held in array A, into ascending numerical order. Use only *one* array which is *just* large enough to hold the maximum number of numbers that may be input. The logic of the method is shown in Figure 8.1. This involves pushing the highest number to the end of the list by exchanging the higher number of each pair working through the list. That is, if element A(1) is greater than element A(2) then their contents are exchanged so that the higher value is in A(2); then the value in A(2) is compared with that in A(3) and exchanged if necessary. The second pass through the list is shorter since at the end of the first pass A(N) contained the highest value in the list and does not need to be compared again. If no exchanges take place during a pass (i.e. E = 0) then the list is in the required sorted order and no further passes are necessary.

Output the list of numbers in its original order and after it has been sorted. Use the following data, and create your own data, to provide a variety of different lists to be sorted.

Data:

15, 12, 3, 20, 22, 22, 9, 4, 23, 2, 0, −25, 17, 18

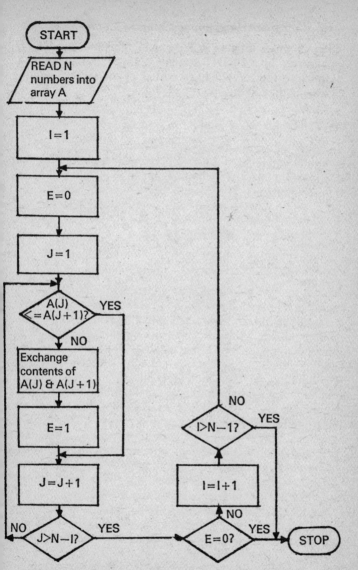

Figure 8.1 Sorting a list of numbers into ascending order

The program is listed in Table A15. This uses the HOME character in a PRINT statement (line 200) to take the cursor to the top left-hand corner of the screen, without clearing the screen.

9 Subroutines and High Resolution Graphics

9.1 Purpose of subroutines

A subroutine is a sequence of instructions designed to perform one or more specific tasks. The routine may be required more than once in different places in the program. When a routine is written as a subroutine it is incorporated in the main program once. During execution the statement, GOSUB *linenumber*, causes control to pass to the line number specified. Execution continues until a RETURN statement is encountered. Control then passes back to the statement *following* the originating GOSUB statement.

A subroutine can be entered as many times as required and therefore can save the writing of similar instructions in several parts of the program. Apart from the extra program writing, the program usually becomes longer if subroutines are not used. A longer program requires more computer storage, and takes longer to translate into machine code; using subroutines wherever possible generally makes a program more efficient.

Once a subroutine has been developed and tested it may be used in quite different programs, either as it stands or with modifications. If possible, subroutines should be designed to allow them to be used in many different ways without modification. This may be done by building in flexibility.

9.2 Independent development

Another advantage of using subroutines is that they may be developed and tested independently from the program(s) in which they are to be used.

By testing subroutines independently a complex program may be built up more quickly using *proved* subroutines. In addition, if a subroutine has been developed for one program, then it can be tested with suitable test data for use in a different program *before* it is incorporated. However, the final program will need to be tested as a *whole* to ensure that the linkages, i.e. statements between the subroutines (as well as the subroutines), give correct results for every branch of the program. The test data must be comprehensive enough to test *every* instruction in the program, as discussed in Chapter 4.

9.3   Graphs and histograms

If you use a computer to analyse data it is almost certain that at some time you will want to plot the data, or maybe group it into a frequency table. The following sections describe a series of subroutines that allow you to do this.

To allow the subroutines to be compatible we need to standardise some of the variable names. The routines have been written to allow up to 100 data values to be processed. These values will be held in the array V. There is therefore the need for a DIM V(100) in the main program. If the data is to be grouped into a frequency table before, say, printing out a histogram, the variable will be stored in array X and the frequency in array F. A frequency table having a maximum of fifteen class intervals should be adequate for most purposes. Therefore the main program will need a DIM statement containing X(15),F(15).

9.4   Frequency grouping subroutines

Before producing a histogram, or carrying out other forms of analysis, it is often required to group individual data points into class intervals and note the total number of values falling into each interval (i.e. the frequency).

A subroutine to do this is given in Table 9.1. The frequency table so constructed is composed of fifteen class intervals. Any data not included as a result of this constraint is printed out by line 2100. A new run can then be undertaken with the class interval parameters respecified accordingly.

```
2000 PRINT"ENTER SIZE OF"
2005 PRINT"CLASS INTERVAL"
2010 INPUT C
2015 PRINT
2020 PRINT "ENTER LOWER BOUND"
2025 PRINT"OF 1ST. INTERVAL"
2030 INPUT L
2040 FOR I = 1 TO N
2050 FOR J = 1 TO 15
2060 IF V(I) >= (L+(C*J)) THEN 2090
2070 F(J)=F(J)+1
2080 GOTO 2110
2090 NEXT J
2100 PRINT V(I);"NOT COUNTED"
2110 NEXT I
2120 FOR J = 1 TO 15
2130 LET X(J) = L + ((J-.5)*C)
2140 NEXT J
2150 RETURN
```

Table 9.1 Frequency grouping routine

The reason for designing the program in this manner is that a completely automatic parameter setting routine may disguise the presence of a 'rogue' value which, once pointed out, you are happy to ignore.

A subroutine to print out a frequency table is given in Table 9.2. As this subroutine is intended to be independent of the grouping subroutine, the class interval and lower bounds are calculated from the array values of X.

```
3000 PRINT
3010 LET C = X(2) - X(1)
3020 LET L = X(1) - (.5*C)
3030 PRINT"--------------------"
3040 PRINT TAB(4);"X";TAB(14);"F"
3050 PRINT"--------------------"
3060 FOR I=1 TO 15
3070 LET B = L + C*(I-1)
3080 PRINT B;TAB(4);"-";TAB(14);F(I)
3090 NEXT I
3100 PRINT"--------------------"
3110 RETURN
```

Table 9.2 Frequency table routine

Problem 1 – Pastureland frequency table

Write a program incorporating these subroutines to process the data shown in Table 9.3. The output required is a frequency table of the percentage pastureland.

Parish	% amount of pastureland
1	46
2	47
3	63
4	74
5	76
6	26
7	37
8	39
9	35
10	43
11	52
12	59

Table 9.3 Parish data

The program, which gives the output shown in Table 9.4, is listed in Table A16.

X	F
20 –	1
30 –	3
40 –	3
50 –	2
60 –	1
70 –	2
80 –	0
90 –	0
100 –	0
110 –	0
120 –	0
130 –	0
140 –	0
150 –	0
160 –	0

Table 9.4 Frequency table for Problem 2

9.5 Sampling from a frequency distribution

A subroutine is described below that allows a value to be sampled from a frequency distribution. The frequency distribution is contained in the two-dimensional array X. The first dimension contains the variable value, the second dimension contains the cumulative percentage frequency.

To allow the subroutine to be used generally in a variety of programs some standardisation of the array containing the frequency distribution is necessary. The number of class intervals has been set at 10 resulting in the dimensions for the array X being (10,2). Note that, for convenience, the existence of 0 subscripts have been ignored. If a required distribution contains less than ten rows (i.e. class intervals), the final entries in the array will be identical. For example, the data to be sampled, shown in Table 9.5, would be contained in the array X(R,I) as shown in Table 9.6.

Variable	Cumulative % frequency
5	10
10	27
15	42
20	65
25	80
30	100

Table 9.5   Data to be sampled

Any distributions to be used from a main program are established in a similar (10,2) format and array X can be equated to them before entering the subroutine.

		Column subscript, I	
		(,1)	(,2)
	(1,)	5	10
	(2,)	10	27
	(3,)	15	42
	(4,)	20	65
	(5,)	25	80
Row subscript, R	(6,)	30	100
	(7,)	30	100
	(8,)	30	100
	(9,)	30	100
	(10,)	30	100

Table 9.6   Contents of X(R,I)

9.6   Description of subroutine

A flowchart for the subroutine is shown in Figure 9.1 and the listing is given in Table 9.7.

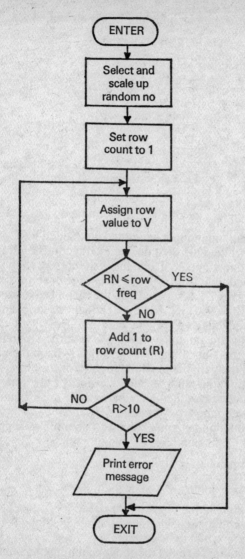

Figure 9.1 Sampling flowchart

```
900 REM SAMPLING SUB
910 LET Z=100*RND(3)
920 FOR R=1 TO 10
930 LET V=X(R,1)
940 IF Z<=X(R,2) THEN 980
950 NEXT R
960 PRINT"ERROR:RN NOT"
965 PRINT"PROPERLY ALLOCATED"
970 END
980 RETURN
```

Table 9.7   Sampling routine

The random number generated is scaled to lie between 0 and 100 (line 910). Within the FOR loop the array X is inspected row by row. The value of the current row variable is assigned to V (line 930) and the value of the scaled random number Z is compared with the current cumulative frequency (line 940). If Z is greater than the frequency the process is repeated for the next row (line 950). When, eventually, the random value Z falls within the current class interval the subroutine is left, carrying back the current value of the variable V. If, due to errors in setting up the distribution, the random value Z cannot be associated with any particular row then lines 960 and 965 are encountered, giving rise to the error message.

A simulation program using this subroutine is given in Chapter 12, section 12.5.

Problem 2 – Input subroutine

Write a subroutine to allow the details of Table 9.5 to be entered into a two-dimensional array D. Make provision for up to ten rows to be entered.

A subroutine to meet the above requirements is shown in Table A17.

9.7 Protected INPUT routine

Input statements can cause the inexperienced user problems. If the return key is pressed in response to an input statement without entering 'data' the VIC accepts a null return and continues through the program, usually with unintended results. The routine to be described (Table 9.8) will not accept solely the return key, thereby preventing 'null' inputs.

```
5000 REM PROTECTED INPUT
5010 ZI$="":ZJ$=""
5020 PRINT"    ";:FOR D=1 TO 300:NEXT
5030 PRINT" ";:FOR D=1 TO 300:NEXT
5040 GET ZI$:IF ZI$="" THEN 5020
5050 IF ZI$<>CHR$(20) THEN 5080
5055 ZL=LEN(ZJ$):IF ZL<1 THEN 5020
5060 ZJ$=LEFT$(ZJ$,ZL-1)
5070 PRINTZI$;:GOTO 5020
5080 IF ZI$=CHR$(13) THEN 5120
5090 PRINTZI$;
5100 ZJ$=ZJ$+ZI$
5110 GOTO 5020
5120 IF ZJ$="" THEN 5020
5130 PRINT
5140 RETURN
```

Table 9.8 Protected input routine

This subroutine makes use of the GET statement which accepts a single character from the keyboard without waiting for the return character. The GET statement allows any entry from the keyboard to be examined by the VIC. You can use this technique, together with the conditional branch statements given in Chapter 5, for writing programs that allow the user to choose a course of action from a 'menu' of choices. Because the GET statement will also accept a 'null' response the user does not have time to respond unless a loop is built into the program. A common method is:

200 GET A$: IF A$ = "" THEN 200

Line 200 forms a closed loop which is only broken by a key being pressed. While the loop in line 200 is being executed no cursor will be displayed.

The principle of the subroutine is that a series of characters keyed in response to a GET loop are concatenated into a string to give the equivalent of the response to an INPUT statement. Line 5010 sets the GET variable ZI$ and the concatenated variable ZJ$ to null strings. A flashing cursor is simulated in lines 5020 and 5030. Lines 5020 to 5040 form therefore a more elaborate GET loop, i.e. 5020 – cursor on; 5030 – cursor off; 5040 – GET character, else cursor on etc. When a character is entered this loop is left and the character tested.

The first test (line 5050) is to check for the delete key (character code 20). If the delete key has been pressed the length of the current string ZJ$ is calculated (line 5055). If ZJ$ is reduced to a null string the entry loop is re-entered, i.e. control is passed to line 5020. Providing ZJ$ does contain characters, line 5060 removes the rightmost character. Line 5070 'prints' the delete character, i.e. causes the cursor to move left and then the GET loop is re-entered.

The second test (line 5080) checks for the pressing of the return key (character 13). Providing the return key has *not* been pressed, the acceptable character is printed and concatenated to ZJ$ in lines 5090 and 5100 before 5110 returns control to the GET loop.

When the return key is pressed, line 5080 causes execution to pass to line 5120 where the status of ZJ$ is checked. If ZJ$ is still a null string then depression of the return key is not acceptable and the GET loop is re-entered. When ZJ$ does contain a response, depression of the return key is 'accepted' and the final PRINT is executed to terminate the action of the trailing semi-colons in previous print statements.

9.8 High resolution graphics

It is possible on the VIC to create user defined characters by switching the individual dots (the pixel) that make up a character on or off. A character is created from an array of 8×8 pixels and so, with suitable programming, graphs can be created to this higher resolution. In order to manipulate characters for this purpose, it is necessary to move some characters from ROM to RAM where they can be suitably amended. This also means that pointers in the memory are adjusted so that the VIC is directed to the appropriate part of RAM. A high resolution cartridge is available for the VIC which extends BASIC with a number of special commands for high resolution work. However, anybody with a VIC which has 3K or more additional memory can achieve high resolution using the following subroutines. A detailed discussion of the requirements is outside the scope of this book but the required routines can be incorporated into user written programs as described below.

```
1000 REM INITIALISATION OF HI-RES
1005 PRINT"■":REM CTRL & BLK
1010 PRINT"⊐":POKE 36879,79
1020 IFPEEK(36869)=253THEN1080
1030 POKE36869,253:POKE36867,PEEK(36867)OR128
1040 POKE55,0:POKE56,19:POKE51,0:POKE52,19
1050 CLR:S=32768:T=5120
1060 PRINT"⊐    INITIALISING"
1070 FORI=0TO255*8+7:POKEI+T,PEEK(I+S):NEXT
1080 REM END OF INITIALISATION
```

Table 9.9 High resolution initialisation

To write a program incorporating high resolution graphics requires the application of two routines. The first routine is given in Table 9.9. This routine, which alters pointers, *must be at the beginning* of the program. Note that this routine also sets the screen, border and character colours (purple, yellow and black); the points are plotted in white. The second routine, given in Table 9.10, plots at a specific pixel on the screen using X and Y as co-ordinates from the top left-hand corner of the screen. This routine can be used as a subroutine as required. An example of the use of these two routines is given in the following section.

```
8000 REM PLOT SUB
8010 X%=X/8:Y%=Y/8:P=X%+Y%*22+7680
8020 Q=PEEK(P):IFQ>=128THEN8050
8030 CN=CN+1:S=5120+(127+CN)*8:T=5120+Q*8
8040 FORI=0TO7:POKES+I,PEEK(T+I):NEXT
8045 Q=127+CN:POKEP,Q
8050 C=5120+Q*8+(YAND7)
8055 POKEC,PEEK(C)OR(2↑(7-(XAND7)))
8060 RETURN
```

Table 9.10 Plot subroutine

9.9 Example of high resolution plotting

The program to be described plots the movement of a confectionary company's shares and the price of cocoa. As eight points can be plotted horizontally within the space of one character, a convenient scale to adopt for business use is two pixel points to a week. This allows 2×52 weeks, i.e. 104 pixels to be used which can be scaled, using traditional graphics characters, into thirteen four-weekly periods. The concept that one year equals thirteen *equal* periods of four weeks is often used in business when data is analysed. Choosing to represent a year over 104 pixels leaves sufficient space across the screen for notation and labelling.

The company's share price is scaled on the left hand axis and the scale for cocoa prices is on the right hand axis. Table 9.11 gives the user routine to be used in conjunction with Tables 9.9 and 9.10. Lines 2000 to 2100 set up the headings and scales, lines 3000 to 3060 plot the company's share prices and lines 4000 to 4060 plot the cocoa prices. The data is placed in lines 6000 to 6122.

```
2000 REM USER SUB
2010 PRINT"⊐"
2020 PRINT"SHARES";TAB(15);"COCOA"
2022 PRINT"PRICE";TAB(15);"PRICE":PRINT:PRINT
2025 READ LB:LT=LB+100:READ RB:RT=RB+100
2030 FOR I=0 TO 10:X=LT-10*I:Y=RT-10*I
2040 X$=RIGHT$("  "+STR$(X),3)
2042 Y$=RIGHT$("  "+STR$(Y),3)
2050 PRINTX$;TAB(17);Y$:NEXT
2058 REM DO VERTICAL AXIS
2060 FORI=5TO15:POKE7680+22*I+3,115:NEXT
2070 POKE7680+15*22+3,91:REM PUT JOIN OF AXES
2078 REM DO HORIZONTAL AXIS
2080 FORI=4TO16:POKE7680+15*22+I,114:NEXT
2088 REM DO VERTICAL AXIS
2090 FORI=5TO15:POKE7680+22*I+16,115:NEXT
2100 PRINT"▓";TAB(3);"1234567890123"
3000 REM 1ST GRAPH
3010 FOR X=28 TO 132
3020 READ D:IF D=0 THEN 3060
3030 Y=INT((LT+55-D)*8/10)
3040 GOSUB 8000
3050 NEXT
3060 REM END 1ST PLOT
4000 REM 2ND GRAPH
4010 FOR X=28 TO 132
4020 READ D:IF D=0 THEN 4060
4030 Y=INT((RT+55-D)*8/10)
4040 GOSUB 8000
4050 NEXT
4060 REM END 2ND GRAPH
5000 GOTO 9000
6000 DATA 60,100
6010 REM 1ST GRAPH
6020 DATA 100,102,105,108,110,115,112,118
6022 DATA 120,122,118,120,120,124,126,130
6024 DATA 128,126,128,126,125,124,126,122
6026 DATA 122,126,128,130,132,136,140,142
6028 DATA 144,142,139,138,136,137,135,138
6030 DATA 136,134,132,132,130,128,130,134
6032 DATA 0
6100 REM 2ND GRAPH
6110 DATA 102,104,110,106,108,110,110,108
6112 DATA 110,112,113,115,118,114,116,118
```

```
6114 DATA 120,122,124,120,118,116,114,110
6116 DATA 110,112,116,118,120,122,124,120
6118 DATA 120,118,118,116,114,113,116,115
6120 DATA 114,110,112,108,106,110,114,116
6122 DATA 0


9000 REM END ROUTINE
9010 PRINT"◼◼◼◼◼◼◼◼◼◼◼◼◼◼◼◼◼◼◼◼◼◼◼◼◼◼◼";
9015 PRINT"PRESS A KEY TO END"
9020 GETA$:IFA$=""THEN9020
9030 END
```

Table 9.11   High resolution plotting example

The majority of the headings and scales are determined
by PRINT statements. However, the start of each vertical
scale is read into LB and RB in line 2025. The appropriate
scale is then calculated. To plot the company's share price
(lines 3000 to 3060), a loop is set up capable of plotting
horizontally from pixel 28 to pixel 132. This loop is left
however if the data value read, D, is zero. Thus as the year
passes only the data statements need extending and to be
terminated with a zero. The value of D is then scaled into
the appropriate pixel value in line 3030. Once the Y value
has been calculated the plotting subroutine (8000) is called
(line 3040).

The plotting of the cocoa price follows a similar logic and
coding. Because the initial routine moves pointers there
will be no cursor on completion of the graph. Therefore a
final short routine (9000) is called which uses a GET to
terminate the program. To prevent the display being spoilt
by the return of the cursor, a series of 'cursor down'
characters precede the message to be printed (in line 9010).
Each cursor down character moves the cursor down one
line on the screen.

10 Sound

10.1 The VIC sound system

The VIC sound system consists of four independent sound generators each having a frequency range of three octaves. Three of the generators give a 'pure' tone while the fourth outputs 'white noise'. White noise is the name given to noise having a wide frequency spectrum. It is used for creating a variety of sound effects, such as explosions, which would be difficult to synthesise from a mixture of three pure tones.

In addition, the system allows the total volume to be program controlled. Because the tones cannot be demonstrated until the volume is turned 'on', this feature will be discussed first.

10.2 Controlling the volume

The sound level is set by POKEing to 36878 a value between 0 and 15. 0 represents the lowest volume level and 15 the loudest. The relative sound level is determined by the volume control setting on the television set being used. Note that the VIC acts on the integer values thereby providing 16 levels of sound (including 0), e.g. POKE 36878,4.99 sets the volume to level 4.

10.3 Controlling the tones

The three pure tone generators are activated by POKEing to 36874, 36875, 36876 and the white noise generator by POKEing 36877. The range of values that can be POKEd is 128 to 255. Values outside this range either have no effect or produce a syntax error. It is convenient, however, to use the value 0 to turn off a particular tone generator. Note that POKEing the same value to locations 36874, 36875, 36876 produces three *different* tones. The tones rise with the values 128 to 254 but value 255 produces a low tone.

```
1000 REM TWO NOTES
1010 POKE 36878,15
1020 FOR N=1 TO 10
1030 POKE 36874,240
1040 FOR S=1 TO 375
1050 NEXT S
1060 POKE 36874,230
1070 FOR S=1 TO 375
1080 NEXT S
1090 NEXT N
1100 POKE 36874,0
1110 POKE 36878,0
1120 RETURN
```

Table 10.1   A two-tone routine

A simple program to alternate two notes is shown in Table 10.1. Line 1010 switches the volume full on. Line 1020 and 1090 causes the two tones to be repeated ten times. Line 1030 'switches on' note value 240 and the FOR loop (lines 1040–1050) provide a delay which determines for how long the note is sustained. The alternate note (value 230) is then similarly sounded and sustained by lines 1060 to 1080. At the end of ten cycles, lines 1100 and 1110 'turn off' the note and volume, respectively.

It is important to terminate any sound routines by statements to 'switch off' the tones used and to return the volume to zero. If this is not done, because POKE is being used, the status of these locations will persist and be carried over into subsequent programs that are run. This is also an important consideration within a program as sound effects are most conveniently incorporated as subroutines. All the programs in this chapter have been written as subroutines and hence have a RETURN statement as the final line.

10.4 Controlling tone and volume

This section uses a more comprehensive version of the previous routine to simulate a passing car siren. The program in Table 10.2 illustrates how the sound level can be varied and the note changed by manipulating variables.

The basic FOR loop is lines 2070 to 2140 and is used to control the sound level. By setting variables X, Y, Z to 1, 15 and 1, respectively, prior to the loop, the sound level is increased at line 2080 (POKE 36878,L) on each pass of the loop from 1 to 15. This causes the sound effect within the loop to become progressively louder. On reaching full volume the loop (lines 2070–2140) is exited and the parameters of the loop are revised over lines 2150, 2160 and 2170 to cause the loop, when next encountered, to decrement L from 15 down to 0. This second pass of the loop is achieved by means of the J loop (lines 2060–2180).

```
2000 REM PASSING SIREN
2010 T=240
2020 D=10
2030 X=1
2040 Y=15
2050 Z=1
2060 FOR J=1 TO 2
2070 FOR L=X TO Y STEP Z
2080 POKE 36878,L
2090 POKE 36875,T
2100 FOR S=1 TO 375
2110 NEXT S
2120 D=-D
2130 T=T+D·
2140 NEXT L
2150 X=15
2160 Y=0
2170 Z=-1
2180 NEXT J
2190 POKE 36875,0
2200 RETURN
```

Table 10.2 A passing siren

In the earlier program (Table 10.1), the two tones were produced by two separate POKE statements and two sets of identical delay loops. For longer programs, alternative programming methods that avoid the repetition of very similar lines of code might be desirable. The current program (Table 10.2) illustrates one of these alternatives to produce two tones.

One of the required tone values is set as T in line 2010 and the difference between the required values is set as D in line 2020. Within the main 'volume control' loop the tone is generated at line 2090 for the duration of the sustain loop (lines 2100–2110). Lines 2120 to 2130 cause the tone value to be revised prior to the next pass. Line 2120 causes the tone difference to be alternately $+D$, $-D$, $+D$, $-D$ etc. on each successive pass. Line 2130 revises the tone value alternately to the two required values. Note on the first pass the variable T is revised *down*, hence the initial value of T (line 2010) needs to be the higher of the two alternatives.

The penultimate line (2190) turns off the tone generator. The volume is already off as the final value of L on exiting the loop is zero.

10.5 Sound effects

The generation of sound effects depends upon software control of the associated parameters. Although there are countless variations possible, the main characteristics to consider are:

a) the frequencies, and their progression over time;
b) the frequency mix;
c) the volume, and its variation over time;
d) the tone-silence ratio.

The frequency can be changed progressively by means of a FOR loop. A downwards progression of frequencies, representing for example, a falling object can be obtained from the program shown in Table 10.3.

```
3000 REM FALLING OBJECT
3010 POKE 36878,15
3020 FOR T=240 TO 130 STEP -1
3030 POKE 36876,T
3040 FOR S=1 TO 30
3050 NEXT S
3060 NEXT T
3070 POKE 36876,0
3080 POKE 36878,0
3090 RETURN
```

Table 10.3 A falling object

A disappearing object can be implied by having the frequencies rise, e.g. by changing the FOR loop at line 3020 to

$$3020 \ FOR \ T = 130 \ TO \ 240$$

Changes in volume have already been illustrated by the passing siren program (Table 10.2). A commonly required sound effect is an explosion. This is achieved by using white noise (i.e. POKE 36877) and allowing it to die away. The program in Table 10.4 illustrates this effect.

```
4000 REM EXPLOSION
4010 POKE 36877,140
4020 FOR L=15 TO 0 STEP -1
4030 POKE 36878,L
4040 FOR S=1 TO 300
4050 NEXT S
4060 NEXT L
4070 POKE 36877,0
4080 RETURN
```

Table 10.4 An explosion

The tone-silence ratio is important for effects representing sounds such as phones. Table 10.5 illustrates a phone ring cycle. The first line (5010) turns the volume full on and

```
5000 REM PHONE RINGING
5010 POKE 36878,15
5020 FOR R=1 TO 5
5030 FOR N=1 TO 2
5040 FOR T=1 TO 20
5050 POKE 36876,238
5060 FOR S=1 TO 5
5070 NEXT S
5080 POKE 36876,0
5090 NEXT T
5100 FOR D=1 TO 150
5110 NEXT D
5120 NEXT N
5130 FOR P=1 TO 1000
5140 NEXT P
5150 NEXT R
5160 POKE 36878,0
5170 RETURN
```

Table 10.5 A phone ring cycle

the last line (5160), prior to RETURN, turns the volume off. The outer FOR loop (lines 5020–5150) repeats the basic sound effect five times. Lines 5030 to 5120 form another FOR loop that produces two 'rings' in quick succession while lines 5130 and 5140 form a relatively long pause before the whole cycle is repeated.

A pure tone is modified in the FOR loop (lines 5040 –5090) to produce a 'ringing' sound. The loop generates 20 bursts of pure tone, each burst being sustained in lines 5060 to 5070 for only a short period.

This chapter has illustrated just a few of the effects that are possible. In all the examples, the progressive change in the FOR loops controlling volume or frequency have been linear. Exponential and other forms of progression can give further effects. Other interesting and unusual effects can be obtained by using the RND function to control volume, frequency and/or timing.

10.6 Problem

Write a program to play the following notes:

G(2), A(2), B(2), G(2), G(2), A(2), B(2), G(2), B(2),
C(2), D(4), B(2), C(2), D(4), D(1), E(1), D(1), C(1),
B(2), G(2), D(1), E(1), D(1), C(1), B(2), G(2), G(2),
lower D(2), G(4), G(2), lower D(2), G(4)

The numbers in brackets indicate the relative duration required for each note. Also practise changing the colour with the notes. The POKE values for musical notes are given in Appendix G. A suitable program is listed in Appendix A18.

11 Using Data Files

11.1 Data files

When a large amount of common data is required by a program it is inconvenient to enter this data each time via the keyboard. A preferable method is to store the data in DATA statements within the program, as described in Chapter 3. However, this is still restrictive as these DATA statements are not readily available to other programs. The most flexible approach is to store your data in separate files from your programs so that the data files may be used by more than one program. You can then also prepare standard programs to analyse and process different data set up in data files.

A data file is created by a BASIC program so that the contents and format are under your control. In practice this means you are likely to write several programs, e.g. one to create the data file, one to update the data file, and some to process the data. This chapter shows how such data files may be created and read.

There are two ways of processing files: sequentially and randomly. Random access of files can only be carried out from disks, whereas sequential access can be carried out from disks or magnetic tape. This book deals only with sequential file systems.

11.2 File records

The contents of a data file may be regarded as the equivalent of a series of DATA statements within a program. Although the data consists of one long 'column' of values, it is useful for you to think and design the logic of your program round the concept of records. For example, a stock record might consist of a stock number, item description, stock level, unit cost and re-order level as shown in Table 11.1.

Stock No	Description	Stock	Unit Cost	Re-order level
1234	Pens	15	45	20
2340	Pencils	50	12	40
2679	Erasers	8	5	10
3456	Rulers	20	26	30
4567	Writing pads	40	35	50
4568	Note books	60	40	30
6770	Labels	70	15	25
6775	Pins	40	15	20
6979	Envelopes	40	20	60
7050	Cash books	30	22	40

Table 11.1 Stock Records

The data contained in Table 11.1, recorded sequentially record by record, would give rise to a 'column' of values as shown below:

> 1234
> PENS
> 15
> 45
> 20
> 2340
> PENCILS
> 50
> etc.

In transferring this data to and from memory it is more convenient to assign separate variable names to each part of a record and move one record at a time. This keeps the program logic simpler, although within a particular program a variable (unit cost, say) may not be manipulated or used.

As the program examples in this chapter use the data

shown in Table 11.1, this is a convenient place to define the variable names to be used:

$$K = \text{stock number}$$
$$D\$ = \text{description}$$
$$S = \text{stock}$$
$$C = \text{unit cost}$$
$$R = \text{re-order level}$$

11.3 OPEN and CLOSE

Any files to be used by your program need to be declared before use. The OPEN statement has the general form:

line number OPEN x, y, z, "filename"

where *x, y, z* are file parameters as follows:

  x = the file number, as chosen by the user for this particular program
  y = the number of the device containing the file
  z = an indicator stipulating whether the file is to be opened to be read, or to be written to

E.g. 10 OPEN 2,1,1,"STOCK"

indicates that a file named "STOCK" will be referred to subsequently as file 2 and is located on device number 1. If *z* =1, this indicates the file is to be written to.

The default option, OPEN *x*, means that the next file encountered will be opened to read only and will be assigned the number *x*.

A separate OPEN statement is required for each file being used. Each file that is opened also needs to be closed after final processing of the file by a CLOSE statement, e.g.

90 CLOSE 1

11.4 File input–output statements

The statement used to output a file has the general form:

PRINT#*filenumber*, *variable list*
e.g. PRINT#1,K,D$,S,C,R

The comma as a delimiter is suppressed so that in the above example K,D$,S,C,R, is written as one string. You can preserve the variables separately by using separate PRINT statements, i.e.

> PRINT#1,K
> PRINT#1,D$
> PRINT#1,S
> PRINT#1,C
> PRINT#1,R

or you can retain the commas by enclosing them in quotes, i.e.

> PRINT#1,K;",";D$;",";S;",";C;",";R

The corresponding read statement is:

> INPUT#1, *filenumber*, *variable list*

Thus a corresponding read statement might be:

> INPUT#1,K,D$,S,C,R

11.5 End of file records

It is convenient if you have within your program your own means of detecting the end of your data. This can easily be done by terminating your data files with a dummy record. The contents of this dummy record are chosen to make it unique. For example, in the stock record file previously discussed the dummy stock number could be made larger than any likely to be encountered, i.e. 9999 if four-digit codes are used.

Since a complete record is transferred as a whole, the remaining fields of the dummy record need to be provided with values as shown below:

> 9999,X,0,0,0

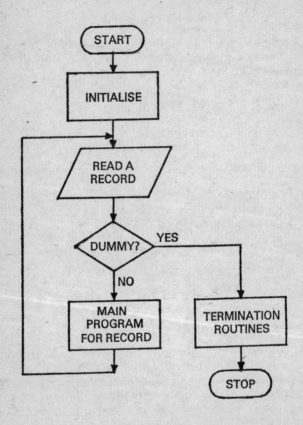

Figure 11.1 General flow with dummy record

The general flow of processing when a dummy record is used is shown in Figure 11.1.

Problem 1 – Stock data file

Write a program to create a stock data file on cassette incorporating a dummy end record for the data in Table 11.1.

A suitable program is listed in Table A19.

Problem 2 – Re-order list

Write a program to read the data file produced in problem 1 and output a list of items to be re-ordered. A sample output is shown in Table 11.2.

RE-ORDER LIST
. . . .

CODE	DESCRIPTION
1234	PENS
2679	ERASERS
3456	RULERS
4567	WRITING PADS
6979	ENVELOPES
7050	CASH BOOKS

Table 11.2 Output from re-order program

A suitable program is listed in Table A20.

Problem 3 – A data file search program

Write a program using string functions to search the stock data file produced in section 11.5 for any stock description containing a specified substring, i.e. PEN. An example of the output is shown in Table 11.3.

STOCK FILE SEARCH
· · · · · · · · · · · · · · · · · · ·

ENTER SEARCH WORD ? PEN
PRESS PLAY ON TAPE#1
OK
· ·

CODE	DETAILS	STOCK
1234	PENS	15
2340	PENCILS	50

· ·

11 RECORDS READ
2 RECORDS LISTED

Table 11.3   Output from search program

The program is listed in Table A21.

12 Applications

12.1 Series

A series consists of a number of terms, each term having a constant relationship to the next term. When devising computer programs for evaluating series, a procedure needs to be designed which allows the next term in the series to be calculated from the previous term.

For example, the exponential series may be evaluated as follows:

$$e^x = 1 + x + \frac{x^2}{2!} + \frac{x^3}{3!} + \ldots \to \infty$$

where $2! = 1 \times 2$ $3! = 1 \times 2 \times 3$ etc.

The steps in the repetitive process to calculate e^x to n terms are:

Step 1. (initialisation), set first term (T) to x, e^x to $1 + T$, and I to 2

Step 2. calculate next term by multiplying previous term by x/I, and add this new term to the old value of e^x

Step 3. repeat step 2 a further $n - 2$ times.

The BASIC routine to calculate e^x is shown in Table 12.1

Problem 1 – Evaluation of cos x

Write a BASIC program for evaluating cos x, given that:

$$\cos x = 1 - \frac{x^2}{2!} + \frac{x^4}{4!} - \frac{x^6}{6!} + \ldots \to \infty$$

The program is listed in Table A22, and the value of cos 30° to 5 terms is given in Appendix B.

```
20 PRINT"NO OF TERMS FOR E↑X"
30 INPUT N
40 PRINT "VALUE OF X";
50 INPUT X
60 LET T=X
70 LET E=1+T
80 FOR I=2 TO N
90 LET T=T*X/I
100 LET E=E+T
110 NEXT I
115 PRINT
120 PRINT"E↑";X;"=";E
125 PRINT"*****************"
130 END
```

Table 12.1 Program to calculate e^x

12.2 Processing experimental data

The program given in Table 12.2 illustrates the use of the computer to process data which is entered at run time from

```
10 PRINT "HEAT OF COMBUSTION"
15 PRINT "-------------------"
20 PRINT "NAME OF SUBSTANCE"
30 INPUT N$
40 PRINT "ENTER S,W,T,R"
50 INPUT S,W,T,R
60 LET H=INT(W*4.2*T*R*0.001/S+0.5)
70 PRINT
80 PRINT"RESULT FOR ";N$
83 PRINT"=";H;"KJ/MOL"
85 PRINT" ***********"
90 PRINT
100 PRINT "ANY MORE DATA"
105 PRINT"(Y=YES,N=NO)"
110 INPUT Y$
120 PRINT
130 IF Y$ = "Y" THEN 20
140 END
```

Table 12.2 'Heat of combustion' problem

the keyboard in response to messages output from the program. This method of working is applicable to, say, a class of students where each group is carrying out similar experiments. The results of the experiments are prepared for input to the computer program, and the program is used to output the final answer for each group. Similarly, a scientist may repeat the same experiments for different substances and the series of results may then be processed by one computer program.

```
HEAT OF COMBUSTION
- - - - - - - - - - - - - - - - - - - - - -
NAME OF SUBSTANCE
? ETHANOL
ENTER S,W,T,R
? .36,100,23.5,46

RESULT FOR ETHANOL
= 1261 KJ/MOL
    *************
ANY MORE DATA
(Y = YES, N = NO)
? Y

NAME OF SUBSTANCE
? METHANOL
ENTER S,W,T,R
? .39,99,21.2,32

RESULT FOR METHANOL
= 723 KJ/MOL
    ************
ANY MORE DATA
(Y = YES, N = NO)
? N
```

Table 12.3   Output from Table 12.2 and data input

The output messages, replies (data input) and results are shown in Table 12.3. S is the mass of substance burnt and W the mass of water heated by the substance in grammes, T is the rise in temperature of the water in °C, and R is the relative molecular mass.

Problem 2 – Roots of quadratic equations

Write a program to calculate the values of the roots of any number of quadratic equations ($ax^2 + bx + c = 0$), given the coefficients a, b and c. If $b^2 - 4ac>0$, output the message 'REAL ROOTS' and the two roots. If $b^2 - 4ac = 0$, output the message 'COINCIDENT ROOTS', and the value $= -b/2a$. If $b^2 - 4ac<0$, output the message

$$3x^2 + 9x + 2 = 0$$
$$7x^2 - 5x + 3 = 0$$
$$x^2 - 8x + 16 = 0$$
$$2x^2 + 3x - 4 = 0$$
$$-3x^2 - 2x + 1 = 0$$
$$x^2 + 2x + 3 = 0$$
$$4x^2 + 4x + 1 = 0$$

Table 12.4   Quadratic equations

'COMPLEX ROOTS'. Allow for interactive entry of a, b and c during run time and stop the execution of the program by zeros being entered for a, b and c. The program is listed in Table A23, and the answers for the equations shown in Table 12.4 are given in Appendix B.

12.3   Tabulation of results and averaging

Measurements, intermediate calculations and final results of experiments may need to be tabulated so that a permanent record is available in an easily readable form. The final answer is often obtained by averaging the results of more than one experiment.

Problem 3 – Width of a slit

The collimator of a spectrometer was used to provide a parallel beam of light from a sodium flame. The beam of light was allowed to fall on a slit placed vertically at the centre of the table of the spectrometer. When appropriate adjustments had been made, parallel bands were seen on looking through the telescope. These were made as sharp as possible by adjusting the slit of the collimator. The crosswires of the eyepiece of the telescope were set on corresponding minima on either side of the centre and the vernier readings were noted; this gave a value of 2A for each of the fringes 1 to 6.

The width of the slit W (cm) = Nλ/A where N is the fringe number, λ = 5.893 × 10^{-5} cm (wavelength of sodium light), and A is in radians.

Write a program to tabulate the measurements taken and values of A and W shown in Table 12.5 (you will need to split the output into two separate tables) and output the average value of the width of the slit. There are two pairs of vernier readings for each fringe number. Values of 2A are found by subtracting the second vernier reading from the first vernier reading. The average value of A is then calculated for each fringe number. The program is listed in Table A24, and the average value of W is given in Appendix B.

FRINGE NUMBER	VERNIER DEG	MIN	READINGS DEG	MIN	A MIN	WIDTH OF SLIT CM
1	41	26	41	20	3	6.75E-2
	221	25	221	19		
2	41	29	41	17		
	221	27	221	15		
3	41	33	41	15		
	221	31	221	13		
4	41	35	41	11		
	221	34	221	10		
5	41	39	41	9		
	221	38	221	8		
6	41	41	41	5		
	221	40	221	4		

Table 12.5   Tabulation of results for Problem 3

12.4 Linear regression

Often straight line graphs may be obtained by manipulating
the formula which defines the relationship between the
variables. The equation of a straight line may be written as,

$$y = mx + c$$

where,

x = the independent variable
y = the dependent variable
m = the slope of the line
c = the intercept of the line on the y axis

A line of 'best fit' can be calculated for a series of data
points from,

$$m = \frac{n\Sigma xy - \Sigma x \Sigma y}{n\Sigma x^2 - (\Sigma x)^2}$$

and $c = \dfrac{\Sigma y - m\Sigma x}{n}$

where,
x and y are the co-ordinates of each data point and
n = number of data points.

There are many equivalent forms of the above expression; some are more suited to manual calculation than
programming. A measure of how closely the data follows
the calculated straight line is given by the coefficient of
correlation (r). If the data lies on a perfectly straight line
then r will be +1 (for positive slope) or −1 (for negative
slope). In the extreme case of no correlation whatsoever,
i.e. the points are scattered randomly, r will equal zero.
The acceptable level of correlation, i.e. value of r, for the
number of readings involved can be found from statistical
tables.

Again, the formulae for r can be presented in different
ways. The expression given below is in a convenient form
for programming when the slope is already evaluated.

$$r = \sqrt{\frac{m(\Sigma xy - \Sigma x \Sigma y/n)}{\Sigma y^2 - (\Sigma y)^2/n}}$$

It should be noted that m, c and r require similar preliminary calculations and that it is convenient to initially calculate and store,

$$\Sigma x, \Sigma y, \Sigma x^2, \Sigma y^2, \Sigma x \Sigma y$$

A program to perform linear regression and calculate r is given in Table 12.6

Problem 4 – Young's modulus of the material of a bar

The bar was clamped horizontally at one end. A weight of mass M (kg) was attached to the other end, and was kept vibrating by an electro-magnet. The vibrating end of the bar was illuminated and was viewed through a slit in a rotating disc, using a telescope. The speed of the disc was gradually increased by adjusting the resistance, placed in series with the electric motor used to rotate the disc, until the bar appeared to be at rest when it was vibrating. A counting arrangement on the motor gave the number of rotations in a definite time.

It can be shown that the motion of the vibrating bar is simple harmonic with a period:

$$T = 2\pi \sqrt{\left(\frac{l^3(M + 33/140m)}{3Yi} \right)}$$

where   i is the moment of inertia of cross-section

Y is Young's modulus of the material of the bar

l is the length of the bar in metres

m is the mass in kg of the vibrating part of the bar

For a bar of rectangular cross-section (breadth b and depth d metres), i = bd³/12.

Hence, $\dfrac{3Ybd^3T^2}{48\,\pi^2 l^3} = M + 33/140m$

T^2 (seconds) plotted for different values of M (kg) gives a straight line graph, and Y may be found using the slope of the graph as follows:

$$Y = \frac{1}{\text{slope of graph}} \quad \frac{16\,\pi^2 l^3}{bd^3}$$

```
50 DIM X(20),Y(20)
60 PRINT "ENTER NO OF"
65 PRINT"PAIRS OF READINGS"
70 INPUT N
80 FOR I = 1 TO N
90 PRINT "ENTER X,Y PAIR ";
100 INPUT X(I),Y(I)
110 NEXT I
120 GOSUB 4000
130 END
4000 LET S1 = 0
4010 LET S2 = 0
4020 LET S3 = 0
4030 LET S4 = 0
4040 LET S5 = 0
4100 FOR I = 1 TO N
4110 LET S1 = S1 + X(I)
4120 LET S2 = S2 + Y(I)
4130 LET S3 = S3 + X(I)↑2
4140 LET S4 = S4 + Y(I)↑2
4150 LET S5 = S5 + X(I)*Y(I)
4160 NEXT I
4170 LET M = (N*S5 - S2*S1)/(N*S3 - S1↑2)
4180 LET C = (S2 - M*S1)/N
4190 LET R = (M *(S5 - S1*S2/N))/(S4 - S2↑2/N)
4192 PRINT
4193 PRINT"Y = M*X + C"
4194 PRINT"M = ";M
4195 PRINT"C = ";C
4196 PRINT
4197 PRINT "COEFF. OF CORR.="
4198 PRINT SQR(R)
4199 RETURN
```

Table 12.6 Linear regression routine

Write a program to output Young's modulus for a bar in Newtons/m². Use the linear regression routine given in

M (kg)	T (seconds)
.097	0.12
.147	0.139
.157	0.145
.177	0.15
.197	0.16

Table 12.7 Data for Problem 4

Table 12.6, to find the slope of the graph for the values of T and M given in Table 12.7. The dimensions of the bar are: b = 1.58 cm, d = 0.312 cm, l = 40 cm. The results are given in Appendix B.

Note: Remember to calculate T^2 for the linear regression 'Y' values; the 'X' values are those listed under M.

12.5 Simulation

12.5.1 *Background*

Simulation requires the writing of a program that models a situation. Changes are brought about in the model, either by the user or by inbuilt routines so that the behaviour of the model can be studied. From studying the behaviour of the model under varying circumstances it is hoped to gain a better understanding of the reality represented by the model.

Some models consist of specific relationships, e.g. a Balance Sheet. In such a case, if you make a change in one variable this leads to a specific revised Balance Sheet. You can, by this means, simulate the effect of changes in labour costs on the profits.

Many forms of simulation require the values of some of the variables to be sampled from a probable range of values. The probable range of values is usually expressed as a probability (or frequency) distribution. In these models, the outcomes and their interactions need to be studied over many simulations to obtain a representative picture of the model's behaviour.

A simple simulation model of this type is discussed below. As the basis of the variability is the sampling from a frequency distribution, the program has been written to make use of the two subroutines previously developed in Chapter 9, section 9.6. Note how the subroutine can be used several times by transferring values to and from the variables common to the subroutine.

12.5.2 *Simulation of combined units*

The problem is to simulate the breakdown pattern of a combined unit comprising a motor assembly and a gear assembly from the breakdown pattern of the individual assemblies.

The running time of a combined unit can be simulated by sampling in turn from the running time distributions of the motor unit and the gear unit. The shorter running time will be the running time of the combined unit. By simulating many such samples the MTBF (mean time between failure) for a combined unit can be obtained.

12.5.3 *Output required*

For a short simulation it is convenient to monitor the course of each pass through the program. Therefore, in this case, the output can be the sampled lives of the motor and gear assemblies, the life of the combined unit and the MTBF to date. For longer simulations this amount of detail would be time consuming to print. It could be incorporated for debugging purposes and then dropped, the final program only producing the ultimate MTBF.

However, a single final statement of the value of the

MTBF is not as informative as a running output of the variable. The decision to terminate a simulation is often taken once the variable under inspection has settled down. These considerations, in this case, lead to the idea that there should be an option to continue the run if the fluctuation in the MTBF is not within the desired limits.

12.5.4 *Description of the program*

The BASIC listing of the main routine is shown in Table 12.8 and of the subroutines in Tables 9.7 and A17 (see Chapter 9).

```
20 DIM M(10,2),G(10,2),D(10,2),X(10,2)
40 GOSUB 800
50 FOR I=1 TO N
52 LET M(I,1)=D(I,1)
54 LET M(I,2)=D(I,2)
56 NEXT I
60 GOSUB 800
70 FOR I=1 TO N
72 LET G(I,1)=D(I,1)
74 LET G(I,2)=D(I,2)
76 NEXT I
80 LET U$="-----------------------"
90 LET T=0
100 LET K=1
115 PRINT
120 PRINT"LENGTH OF SIMULATION"
130 INPUT L
140 PRINT
145 PRINT U$
150 PRINT"SIM";TAB(4);"MTR";TAB(8);"GEAR";
160 PRINTTAB(13);"COMB";TAB(18);"MTBF"
170 PRINT U$
180 FOR S=K TO L
200 FOR I=1 TO 10
202 LET X(I,1)=M(I,1)
204 LET X(I,2)=M(I,2)
206 NEXT I
```

Table 12.8 (1)   Main routine for simulation program

```
210 GOSUB 900
220 LET U1=V
240 FOR I=1 TO 10
242 LET X(I,1)=G(I,1)
244 LET X(I,2)=G(I,2)
246 NEXT I
250 GOSUB 900
260 LET U2=V
280 LET C=U1
290 IF U2>U1 THEN 320
300 LET C=U2
320 LET T=T+C
330 LET A=T/S
335 LET A=INT(10*A)/10
340 PRINTS;TAB(4);U1;TAB(8);U2;TAB(13);C;TAB(17);
350 NEXT S
355 PRINT U$
370 LET K=L+1
380 PRINT"ENTER ADDITIONAL"
390 PRINT"SIMULATIONS REQUIRED,"
395 PRINT"OR ZERO TO STOP"
400 INPUT L
405 IF L>0 THEN 420
410 END
420 LET L=K+L-1
430 GOTO 170
```

Table 12.8 (2)   Main routine for simulation program

The motor unit frequency distribution is input after
control is transferred to the subroutine from line 40. The
input is returned in array D and the contents copied to array
M. This allows array D and hence the subroutine to be used
again. This time the gear unit frequency distribution is
input and on return to the main routine it is copied from
array D to array G.

The next stage of the program initialises the variables T
and K in readiness for the simulation. Variable T is the

cumulative combined unit running time, and variable K is the starting (or continuation) value of the simulation count. K is initially set at one for the first run (line 100) and is revised in line 370 in case the FOR loop is to be continued.

The initial length of the simulation is input at line 130. Line 150 and 160 print the required heading. PRINT U$ produces a line of dashes and is used to highlight the headings (lines 145 and 170). Each line of calculated output is produced within the FOR loop from lines 180 to 350.

To sample from the motor unit distribution (array M) it is copied to array X by lines 200–206. The subroutine starting at line 900 is entered and a sample from array X is returned as variable V. In line 220 this value is retained for future reference as variable U1. This procedure is then repeated for the gear unit, the sampled value being retained as U2. Lines 280–300 carry forward the lower of the two values as variable C (this is the running time of the combined unit). The cumulative running time is calculated in line 320 and the current average running time (the MTBF) is calculated in line 330 as A. Having completed a pass through the FOR loop, a line of output provides the current simulated values of U1, U2, C and A.

After simulating the stipulated number of times (i.e. L), the FOR loop is left. In anticipation of continuing, the value of K is reset in line 370. Lines 390–400 allow you to reset L, or, if you enter zero, the run stops.

To separate this interactive part of the run from the previously calculated output, PRINT U$ is now used in line 355. If the run is to be continued, control is returned to line 170 to separate the subsequent output in a similar way. This means of trying to keep the output tidy is best appreciated by studying extracts from a run of this program as shown in Table 12.9.

LENGTH OF SIMULATION
? 10

....

SIM	MTR	GEAR	COMB	MTBF
1	16	18	16	16
2	16	14	14	15
3	8	16	8	12.6
4	16	18	16	13.5
5	16	14	14	13.6
6	8	14	8	12.6
7	12	22	12	12.5
8	20	22	20	13.5
9	16	10	10	13.1
10	4	14	4	12.1

....

ENTER ADDITIONAL
SIMULATIONS REQUIRED,
OR ZERO TO STOP ? 5

....

11	16	14	14	12.3
12	12	14	12	12.3
13	16	18	16	12.6
14	16	16	16	12.8
15	12	18	12	12.8

....

ENTER ADDITIONAL
SIMULATIONS REQUIRED,
OR ZERO TO STOP ? 0

Table 12.9   Example of output from Table 12.8

Problem 5 – Combined units simulation

Use the simulation program (Table 12.8) to calculate the
mean time between failure for a combined unit consisting
of motor and gear units having the failure pattern shown in
Table 12.10. Simulate 100 failures. The answer is given in
Appendix B.

Motor Unit		Gear Unit	
Life (weeks)	Cum % Freq	Life (weeks)	Cum % Freq
4	20	10	10
8	40	12	15
12	50	14	40
16	90	16	60
20	100	18	75
		20	80
		22	100

Table 12.10 Failure pattern of units

12.6 Financial

Many financial calculations relate to the calculation of interest over a period of time. A common example involving repayment of interest (and capital) is a mortgage repayment. Once a mortgage has been obtained there is little you can do about the repayments required. A computer program, however, could be particularly useful in examining the effects of changing the variables to assist in choosing the most suitable mortgage.

12.6.1 *Mortgage calculations*

The repayments required on a mortgage can be calculated from the following formula:

$$R = \frac{Pi(1 + i)^n}{(1 + i)^n - 1}$$

where,

P = Principal (the amount borrowed)
n = duration of mortgage
i = interest rate per annum
R = required annual repayment

Many organisations providing mortgages allow you to repay monthly. The monthly repayments are usually $\frac{1}{12}$ of the annual repayments because they are regarded as simply advance payments of the annual premium. These monthly advance payments do not themselves earn interest.

12.6.2 *Requirements of the program*

In examining alternative mortgage proposals you would want to change P, n and/or i as required. As successive changes were made it would be useful to be reminded as to the current values of these three variables.

This program is the type likely to be used by someone such as a broker in a working environment. As he is not likely to have any programming knowledge the PRINT messages need to be clear and the data entered in the most natural way. Thus the variables to be revised are indicated by entering I, P or N rather than entering a numeric alternative such as 1, 2 or 3. Although the program is slightly more complex as a result, this is regarded as a secondary consideration.

The input to the program is straightforward; the interest rate is entered as a percentage (i.e. 12.5 not .125) as this is how it is commonly quoted.

12.6.3 *Description of the program*

A listing of the program is given in Table 12.11 and an example of the output in Table 12.12.

Line 30 defines the function FNM which rounds to two decimal places thereby representing monetary amounts to the nearest pence. Lines 40–100 request the starting values of I, P and N. The annual repayment is calculated in line 120 and printed as a monthly repayment in line 130. A blank line (line 140) is printed before looping and producing revised output.

Line 160 allows you to revise optionally the values of I, P or N and line 170 reminds you of the current values. The option you enter is identified by the program over lines 200–250. If an inappropriate character is entered this char-

```
10 REM MORTGAGE REPAYMENT
30 DEF FNM(X)=INT(X*100 + .5)/100
40 PRINT"INTEREST RATE AS A %"
50 INPUT I
60 LET I = I/100
70 PRINT"SIZE OF MORTGAGE"
80 INPUT P
90 PRINT"PERIOD OF LOAN (YRS)"
100 INPUT N
120 LET R=(P*I*(1+I)↑N)/(((1+I)↑N)-1)
130 PRINT"MONTHLY REPAYMENTS ="
135 PRINT FNM(R/12)
140 PRINT
160 PRINT"ENTER I,P OR N"
165 PRINT"TO REVISE INTEREST,"
167 PRINT"PRINCIPAL OR YEARS"
170 PRINT:PRINT"EXISTING VALUES ARE"
175 PRINT I;P;N
180 PRINT:PRINT"OR ENTER S TO STOP"
190 INPUT A$
200 IF A$ = "S" THEN 350
210 PRINT"REVISED VALUE"
220 INPUT X
230 IF A$ = "I" THEN 290
240 IF A$ = "P" THEN 310
250 IF A$ = "N" THEN 330
260 PRINT:PRINT"REVISION ERROR:"
270 PRINT A$;" ENTERED":PRINT
280 GOTO 160
290 LET I = X/100
300 GOTO 120
310 LET P = X
320 GOTO 120
330 LET N = X
340 GOTO 120
350 END
```

Table 12.11 Program for mortgage calculation

acter 'falls through' these lines and the error message (line 260) is printed. Otherwise the revised value entered in line 220 is assigned accordingly over lines 290 to 330. The program then loops back to line 120 to recalculate R.

```
               INTEREST RATE AS A %
               ? 12.5
               SIZE OF MORTGAGE
               ? 10000
               PERIOD OF LOAN (YRS)
               ? 25
               MONTHLY REPAYMENTS =
                109.95

               ENTER I,P OR N
               TO REVISE INTEREST,
               PRINCIPAL OR YEARS

               EXISTING VALUES ARE
                .125      10000      25

               OR ENTER S TO STOP
               ? P
               REVISED VALUE
               ? 8000
               MONTHLY REPAYMENTS =
                87.96

               ENTER I,P OR N
               TO REVISE INTEREST,
               PRINCIPAL OR YEARS

               EXISTING VALUES ARE
                .125      8000       25

               OR ENTER S TO STOP
               ? S
```

Table 12.12   Example of output from Table 12.11

Problem 6 – Monthly repayments

Run the program shown in Table 12.11 using the following data:

   Interest rate, 11%
   Loan, £15,000
   Period of loan, 20 years

Then revise the loan to £20,000. The two monthly repayments are given in Appendix B.

12.7 Morse trainer

This program makes use of the VIC's sound facilities to 'playback' in Morse code any string entered at the keyboard. In addition, an appropriate graphics dot or dash is displayed on the screen to match the Morse sounds.

The program is given in Table 12.13. Line 5 sets the tone to be sounded for the Morse signal and line 6 sets the basic unit of sustain used in subsequent delay loops. By making S smaller, the Morse will be played quicker but the *relative* timings of dots, dashes and pauses will be maintained. Line 20 transfers control to subroutine 400 which sets up an array M$(26) with strings of dots and dashes to represent the Morse code (in alphabetic sequence). This routine could be extended to include the full Morse code set by increasing the array size and adding suitable DATA statements.

```
4 DIM M$(26),L$(40)
5 POKE 36876,241
10 S=10
14 PRINT"◧◨◨◧"
15 PRINT"    MORSE TRAINER"
16 PRINT"    -------------    ◧◨◧◧"
20 GOSUB 400
25 PRINT"◧ENTER MESSAGE ◧";
30 INPUT S$
35 PRINT"◧◨"
40 GOSUB 500
50 FOR K=1 TO L
60 L$ = L$(K)
70 GOSUB 1000
90 NEXT K
100 END
400 FOR I= 1 TO 26
410 READ M$(I)
420 NEXT I
430 DATA ".-","-...","-.-.","-..","."
440 DATA "..-.","--.","....","..",".---"
450 DATA "-.-",".-..","--","-.","---"
```

```
460 DATA ".--.","--.-",".-.","...","-"
470 DATA "..-","...-",".--","-..-","-.--"
480 DATA "--.."
490 RETURN
500 REM TRANSLATE
510 L=LEN(S$)
520 FOR I=1 TO L
525 L$(I)=CHR$(32)
530 FOR J=1 TO 26
540 IF MID$(S$,I,1)<>CHR$(64+J) THEN 550
545 L$(I)=M$(J)
550 NEXT J
560 NEXT I
1000 REM SOUND CHARACTER
1010 IF L$<>CHR$(32) THEN 1030
1020 GOSUB 7000:GOTO 1100
1030 W=LEN(L$)
1040 FOR I=1 TO W
1050 X$=MID$(L$,I,1)
1060 IF X$=CHR$(46) THEN GOSUB 4000
1070 IF X$=CHR$(45) THEN GOSUB 5000
1080 NEXT I
1090 GOSUB 6000
1100 RETURN
4000 REM DOT
4005 PRINT"●";
4010 FOR D=1 TO S:POKE 36878,15:NEXT D
4040 FOR D=1 TO S:POKE 36878,0:NEXT D
4070 RETURN
5000 REM DASH
5005 PRINT"■ ";
5010 FOR D=1 TO 3*S:POKE 36878,15:NEXT D
5040 FOR D=1 TO S:POKE 36878,0:NEXT D
5070 RETURN
6000 REM END LETTER
6005 PRINT
6010 FOR D= 1 TO 2*S:POKE 36878,0:NEXT D
6040 RETURN
7000 REM END WORD
7005 PRINT
7010 FOR D= 1 TO 6*S:POKE 36878,0:NEXT D
7040 RETURN
```

Table 12.13 Morse trainer

The message to be transmitted in Morse is input at line 30. This is examined character by character in the subroutine (lines 500–560) and as each character is identified in line 540 its Morse code equivalent (M$(J)) is copied to array L$. Each character occupies one cell in the array. The dimension statement (line 4) therefore limits the current program to messages of 40 characters.

Lines 50 to 90 in the main program then transfer the Morse code string from *array* L$ to the *variable* L$ within a loop. The current content of the *variable* L$ then is used by the subroutine 1000 to 1100 to determine which sound subroutines should be called.

If L$ is a space then the 'end word' subroutine (lines 7000–7040) is entered. Lines 4000 to 4070 or lines 5000 to 5070 are executed if L$ is a dot or dash, respectively. Having sounded appropriately, the 'end letter' subroutine (lines 6000–6040) is entered.

The relative timing is determined by the delay loops in the sound subroutines. Taking the dot character as a unit of duration, the time interval between characters is also equivalent to a dot. The duration of a dash is three dots. Between letters there is a pause equivalent to three dots, but as the last dot or dash has a pause of one unit within its own subroutine the 'end letter' subroutine needs to add only two dot equivalents. Similarly, as the interval between words is equivalent to *seven* dots the subroutine (lines 7000–7040) adds a further pause equivalent to *six* dots. These timings are approximate because the time spent in the rest of the program will add a small fixed element.

The above program can be modified in several ways; for example by making the INPUT from tape, practice tapes could be compiled by someone else so that the listener does not already know the message.

Appendix A
Programs (Tables A1 to A24)

```
20 INPUT A,E,P,N,R
25 PRINT
30 LET T=((A+E)*N+P)/R
40 PRINT"LENGTH OF STAY:"
45 PRINT N;"NIGHTS"
50 PRINT"ACCOMODATION:"
55 PRINT"$";A;"PER NIGHT"
60 PRINT"EXPENSES(MEALS ETC.):"
65 PRINT"$";E
70 PRINT"ALLOWANCE(PRESENTS):"
75 PRINT"$";P
80 PRINT "EXCHANGE RATE:"
85 PRINT R;"($ TO THE £)"
86 PRINT
90 PRINT "£ REQUIRED:"
95 PRINT T
100 PRINT"*******"
110 END
```

Table A1 Number of £s required

```
20 INPUT N,F,P,S,D
25 PRINT
30 LET C=N*(F+P+2*S*(100-D)/100)/100
40 PRINT"NO OF DELEGATES:"
45 PRINT N
50 PRINT"COST OF FOLDERS:"
55 PRINT F;"P EACH"
60 PRINT"COST OF PAPER:"
65 PRINT P;"P PER PAD"
70 PRINT"COST OF PENS LESS";D;"%:"
75 PRINT S;"P EACH"
80 PRINT
85 PRINT"COST OF STATIONERY ="
90 PRINT"£";C
95 PRINT"*******"
100 END
```

Table A2 Cost of stationery

```
20 PRINT"CALCULATIONS FOR"
21 PRINT"DIFFERENT CODES"
25 PRINT"----------------"
30 PRINT
40 REM N=NUMBER OF
45 REM SETS OF DATA
50 INPUT N
60 FOR I=1 TO N
70 INPUT C,X,Y
80 ON C GOTO 90,100,110,120,130
90 LET R=X+Y
95 GOTO 140
100 LET R=X-Y
105 GOTO 140
110 LET R=X*Y
115 GOTO 140
120 LET R=X/Y
125 GOTO 140
130 LET R=X↑Y
140 PRINT"CODE:";C;"R =";R
145 PRINT"*****************"
150 PRINT
160 NEXT I
170 END
```

Table A3 Using the ON . . . GOTO statement

```
5 PRINT"ENTER WIDTH,DEPTH"
10 INPUT W,D
15 LET S=11-INT(W/2+0.5)
20 PRINT"⬚":REM CLEAR
25 FOR I=1 TO 11-INT(D/2+0.5)
30 PRINT
35 NEXT I
40 PRINT TAB(S);"Γ";
45 FOR I=1 TO W-2
50 PRINT"⁻";
55 NEXT I
60 PRINT"⌐"
65 FOR I=1 TO D-2
70 PRINT TAB(S);"I ";TAB(W-1+S);" I"
75 NEXT I
80 PRINT TAB(S);"L";
85 FOR I=1 TO W-2
90 PRINT"_";
95 NEXT I
100 PRINT"⅃"
105 END
```

Table A4   Centering a rectangle

```
61 PRINT"⬚":REM CLEAR
63 PRINT"OPTION H,N,L OR F";
64 INPUT P$
65 IF P$="F" THEN 380
66 IF P$="N" THEN 130
67 IF P$="L" THEN 291
```

Table A5   Print options (amendments to Table 2.1)

```
70 REM LETTER HEADING
71 PRINT"NO OF SHEETS"
72 PRINT"& PRINT POSITION"
73 INPUT N1,P
74 FOR I=1 TO N1
75 PRINT"⌑":REM CLEAR
76 PRINT
77 PRINT
80 PRINT TAB(P);A$
90 PRINT TAB(P);B$
100 PRINT TAB(P);C$
110 PRINTTAB(P);D$
111 END
112 NEXT I
115 GOTO 61
```

Table A6 Letter headings (amendments to Table 2.1)

```
120 REM NOTEBOOK LABEL
130 PRINT"ENTER NO OF LABELS"
135 PRINT"& NAME LENGTH"
140 INPUT N2,L
145 PRINT"ENTER NO OF LABELS"
150 PRINT"PER PAGE"
151 INPUT N3
152 FOR I=1 TO N2/N3
153 PRINT"⊐":REM CLEAR
154 FOR J=1 TO N3


200 PRINT"*                    *"
210 PRINT"*                    *"
220 LET J1=INT(10-L/2)
221 PRINT"*";
223 FOR I1=1 TO J1
224 PRINT" ";
225 NEXT I1
226 PRINT N$;
230 PRINT TAB(21);"*"
235 PRINT"*                    *"
240 PRINT"*                    *"


281 NEXT J
282 NEXT I
283 GOTO 61
```

Table A7 Notebook labels (amendments to Table 2.1)

```
290 REM ENVELOPE LABEL
291 PRINT"ENTER NO OF LABELS"
292 PRINT"PER PAGE & TOTAL"
293 INPUT N5,N6
294 FOR I=1 TO N6/N5
295 PRINT"⌂":REM CLEAR
296 FOR J=1 TO N5
```

```
374 NEXT J
375 END
376 NEXT I
378 GOTO 61
```

Table A8 Envelope labels (amendments to Table 2.1)

```
5 PRINT"ℸ":REM CLEAR
10 SM=7680:CM=38400
20 S=SM+22*8+8
30 C=CM+22*8+8
40 FOR I=0 TO 5
50 FOR J=0 TO 5
60 READ X
70 POKE S+22*I+J,X
80 POKE C+22*I+J,6
90 NEXT J
100 NEXT I
110 X=74:Y=75:CL=6
115 XA=85:YA=73
120 FOR I=1 TO 10
130 POKE S+22*4+2,X
140 POKE C+22*4+2,CL
150 POKE S+22*4+3,Y
160 POKE C+22*4+3,CL
170 FOR D=1 TO 1000:NEXT D
180 XB=X:X=XA:XA=XB
185 YB=Y:Y=YA:YA=YB
190 NEXT I
200 DATA 85,102,102,102,102,73
210 DATA 93,87,96,96,87,93
220 DATA 93,96,85,73,96,93
230 DATA 93,96,74,75,96,93
240 DATA 93,96,96,96,96,93
250 DATA 74,64,64,64,64,75
260 END
```

Table A9 Animated face

```
20 PRINT "SIDES OF TRIANGLE";
30 INPUT A,B,C
40 LET X=(A*A+C*C-B*B)/(2*A*C)
50 LET R=B/(2*SIN(ATN(SQR(1-X*X)/X)))
60 PRINT
70 PRINT "RADIUS =";R;"M"
75 PRINT "********************"
80 END
```

Table A10   Radius of circumcircle

```
10 DEF FNR(X)=INT(X/0.1+0.5)*0.1
20 DEF FND(U)=ATN(1)*4/180
30 PRINT"THREE SIDES AND ANGLE"
40 PRINT"0 IF UNKNOWN"
50 INPUT A,B,C,D1:PRINT
60 IF A<0 THEN 230
70 IF D1>0 THEN 110
80 LET S=(A+B+C)/2
90 LET R=FNR(SQR(S*(S-A)*(S-B)*(S-C)))
100 GOTO 190
110 LET D=D1*FND(U)
120 IF A=0 THEN 160
130 IF B=0 THEN 180
140 LET R=FNR((A*B*SIN(D))/2)
150 GOTO 190
160 LET R=FNR((B*C*SIN(D))/2)
170 GOTO 190
180 LET R=FNR((A*C*SIN(D))/2)
190 PRINT"AREA =";R;"SQ CM"
200 PRINT"**********************"
210 PRINT
220 GOTO 30
230 END
```

Table A11   Areas of triangles

```
10 DATA CUBOID,CYLINDER,"HEX BAR"
20 DEF FNR(A)=INT(A/F+0.5)*F
30 DEF FNP(U)=ATN(1)*4
40 PRINT "ENTER CODE AND SCALE"
50 INPUT C,F
60 IF C = 0 THEN 250
70 PRINT "ENTER TWO DIMENSIONS"
75 INPUT D1,D2
80 PRINT "ENTER HEIGHT"
85 INPUT H
90 PRINT
100 ON C GOTO 110,130,150
110 LET A=D1*D2
120 GOTO 160
130 LET A=FNP(U)*D1*D1
140 GOTO 160
150 LET A=SQR(27)/2*D1*D1
160 FOR I=1 TO C
170 READ N$
180 NEXT I
190 PRINT "VOL OF ";N$;" ="
195 PRINT FNR(A*H);" CUBIC CM"
200 PRINT "**********************"
210 PRINT
220 PRINT
230 RESTORE
240 GOTO 40
250 END
```

Table A12   Volumes of solids

```
20 INPUT N
30 DIM A(20),B(20)
40 FOR I=1 TO N
50 READ A(I)
60 NEXT I
70 FOR I=1 TO N STEP 5
90 FOR J=I TO I+4
100 LET B(J)=A(N+1-J)
110 PRINT B(J);
130 NEXT J
140 PRINT
150 NEXT I
160 DATA 1,2,3,4,5,6,7,8,9,10,11,12,13
170 DATA 14,15,16,17,18,19,20
180 END
```

Table A13   Copying an array

```
20 DIM A(5,5)
30 INPUT M
40 IF M=0 THEN 260
50 LET D=0
60 FOR I=1 TO M
70 FOR J=1 TO M
80 READ A(I,J)
90 PRINT A(I,J);
100 NEXT J
110 PRINT
120 D=D+A(I,I)+A(I,M+1-I)
130 NEXT I
140 PRINT
150 IF M/2=INT(M/2) THEN 180
160 LET N=INT(M/2)+1
170 LET D=D-A(N,N)
180 PRINT"SUM ON DIAGONALS ="
185 PRINT D
190 PRINT
200 PRINT
210 RESTORE
220 GOTO 30
230 DATA 10,11,12,13,14,15,16,17,18,19
240 DATA 20,21,22,23,24,25,26,27,28,29
250 DATA 30,31,32,33,34
260 END
```

Table A14   Sum of elements

```
20 INPUT N
30 PRINT"⊐":REM CLEAR
40 DIM A(14)
50 FOR I=1 TO N
60 READ A(I):PRINT A(I)
70 NEXT I
80 PRINT
90 FOR I=1 TO N-1
100 LET E=0
110 FOR J=1 TO N-1
120 IF A(J)<=A(J+1) THEN 170
130 LET S=A(J)
140 LET A(J)=A(J+1)
150 LET A(J+1)=S
160 LET E=1
170 NEXT J
180 IF E=0 THEN 200
190 NEXT I
200 PRINT"█":REM HOME
210 FOR K=1 TO N
220 PRINT TAB(10);A(K)
230 NEXT K
240 DATA 15,12,3,20,22,22,9,4,23,2,0,-25,17,18
250 END
```

Table A15 Sorting a list of numbers

```
20 DIM V(100),X(15),F(15)
30 PRINT "ENTER NO OF PARISHES"
40 INPUT N
50 PRINT
60 FOR I = 1 TO N
70 PRINT "PARISH";I
80 INPUT V(I)
90 NEXT I
100 PRINT
110 GOSUB 2000
120 GOSUB 3000
125 END
```

Table A16 Pastureland frequency table

```
800 PRINT
810 PRINT"NO OF ROWS"
815 PRINT"IN FREQ DIST."
820 INPUT N
830 IF N<11 THEN 850
840 PRINT"NOT MORE THAN 10"
842 PRINT"TRY AGAIN"
845 GOTO 800
850 PRINT
860 PRINT"INPUT X & CUM FREQ"
870 FOR I=1 TO N
880 INPUT D(I,1),D(I,2)
890 NEXT I
899 RETURN
```

Table A17   Input subroutine

```
10 PRINT"XXXXXXXXXXXXXXXXXXXXX";
20 READ T$
30 PRINTT$
40 READ N,S
50 POKE 36878,15
60 IF N<0 THEN 130
70 POKE 36876,N
80 FOR D=1 TO 20*S
90 POKE 36879,N-25
100 NEXT D
110 POKE 36876,0
120 GOTO 40
130 POKE 36878,0
140 POKE 36879,27
150 END
200 DATA "FRERE JACQUES"
210 DATA 172,2,181,2,189,2,172,2
220 DATA 172,2,181,2,189,2,172,2
230 DATA 189,2,193,2,200,4
240 DATA 189,2,193,2,200,4
250 DATA 200,1,206,1,200,1,193,1,189,2,172,2
260 DATA 200,1,206,1,200,1,193,1,189,2,172,2
270 DATA 172,2,145,2,172,4
280 DATA 172,2,145,2,172,4
290 DATA -1,-1
```

Table A18   A simple tune

```
30 OPEN 1,1,1,"STK-DATA"
210 INPUT K,D$,S,C,R
215 PRINT#1,K
216 PRINT#1,D$
217 PRINT#1,S
218 PRINT#1,C
219 PRINT#1,R
230 IF K=9999 THEN 250
240 GOTO 210
250 CLOSE 1
600 END
```

Table A19 Stock data file creation

```
30 OPEN 1,1,0,"STK-DATA"
40 PRINT"RE-ORDER LIST"
45 PRINT"-------------"
50 PRINT
60 PRINT"CODE";TAB(7);"DESCRIPTION"
65 PRINT"----";TAB(7);"-----------"
70 PRINT
80 INPUT#1,K,D$,S,C,R
90 IF K=9999 THEN 130
100 IF S>R THEN 80
110 PRINT K;TAB(7);D$
120 GOTO 80
130 CLOSE 1
140 END
```

Table A20 Re-order list

```
1 PRINT "⌂"
2 PRINT"STOCK FILE SEARCH"
4 PRINT"-----------------"
5 PRINT
6 PRINT"ENTER SEARCH WORD"
10 INPUT X$
15 L=LEN(X$)
20 OPEN 1,1,0,"STK-DATA"
22 LET E = 0
24 LET F = 0
25 LET U$ ="-----------------------"
27 PRINT U$
28 PRINT TAB(1);"CODE";TAB(6);
   "DETAILS";TAB(15);"STOCK
29 PRINTU$
30 INPUT#1,K,D$,S,C,R
35 LET E = E + 1
40 LET W=LEN(D$)-L+1
50 IF K= 9999 THEN 800
60 FOR I=1TO W
70 LET Z$=MID$(D$,I,L)
80 IF Z$=X$ THEN 100
90 NEXT I
92 GOTO 30
100 LET F = F + 1
110 PRINT K;TAB(6);D$;TAB(15);S
140 GOTO 30
800 CLOSE 1
801 PRINT U$
805 PRINT E ;"RECORDS READ"
810 PRINT F ;"RECORDS LISTED"
950 END
```

Table A21   Stock file search

```
20 PRINT"NO OF TERMS FOR COS X"
30 INPUT N
40 PRINT"VALUE OF X (DEGREES)"
50 INPUT X1
60 LET X=(X1*ATN(1)*4/180)↑2
70 LET T=1
80 LET C=1
90 FOR I=2 TO N*2 STEP 2
100 LET T=(-1)*T*X/((I-1)*I)
105 LET C=C+T
110 NEXT I
115 PRINT
120 PRINT"COS";X1;"=";C
125 PRINT"*******************"
130 END
```

Table A22   Cos X

```
10 DEF FNR(A)=INT(A/0.01+0.5)*0.01
20 PRINT"ROOTS OF"
25 PRINT"QUADRATIC EQUATIONS"
30 PRINT"-------------------"
40 PRINT"ENTER A,B,C"
50 PRINT"(ZEROES TO STOP)"
60 INPUT A,B,C
70 IF A=0 THEN 210
80 LET D=B*B-4*A*C
90 IF D<0 THEN 150
100 IF D=0 THEN 170
110 LET D=SQR(D)
120 PRINT"REAL ROOTS:"
125 PRINT FNR((-B+D)/(2*A));
130 PRINT"AND ";FNR((-B-D)/(2*A))
140 GOTO 180
150 PRINT"COMPLEX ROOTS"
160 GOTO 180
170 PRINT"COINCIDENT ROOTS:";
175 PRINT FNR(-B/(2*A))
180 PRINT"*********************"
190 PRINT
200 GOTO 40
210 END
```

Table A23   Roots of quadratic equations

```
10 INPUT"WAVELENGTH";L
20 INPUT"NO OF FRINGES";N
30 PRINT"ENTER TWO SETS OF"
40 PRINT"VERNIER READINGS"
50 PRINT"FOR EACH FRINGE"
60 PRINT"IN DEG & MIN"
70 FOR I=1 TO N
80 FOR J=1 TO 2
90 INPUT P(I,J),Q(I,J),R(I,J),S(I,J)
100 LET B(J)=ABS(P(I,J)*60+Q(I,J)-R(I,J)
    *60-S(I,J))
110 NEXT J
120 LET A(I)=INT((B(1)+B(2))/4)
130 LET W(I)=I*L*60*180/(A(I)*ATN(1)*4)
140 NEXT I
150 PRINT
160 PRINT"FRINGE    READINGS"
170 PRINT"NUMBER DEG MIN DEG MIN"
180 PRINT"————————————————————"
190 FOR I=1 TO N
200 PRINT TAB(5);P(I,1);TAB(10);Q(I,1);
210 PRINT TAB(14);R(I,1);TAB(19);S(I,1)
220 PRINT TAB(2);I
230 PRINT TAB(5);P(I,2);TAB(10);Q(I,2);
240 PRINT TAB(14);R(I,2);TAB(19);S(I,2)
250 PRINT"————————————————————"
260 NEXT I
270 PRINT:END
280 PRINT"FRINGE   A  WIDTH OF"
290 PRINT"NUMBER MIN SLIT  CM"
300 PRINT:PRINT"————————————————————"
310 FOR I=1 TO N
320 LET W(I)=INT(W(I)/0.0001+0.5)*0.0001
330 PRINT:PRINT
340 PRINT TAB(2);I;TAB(7);A(I);TAB(12);W(I)
350 PRINT:PRINT
360 PRINT"————————————————————"
370 PRINT:LET W=W+W(I)
380 NEXT I
390 PRINT:END:LET W=INT(W/N/0.0001+0.5)*0.0001
400 PRINT"SLIT WIDTH =";W;" CM"
410 PRINT"*********************"
420 END
```

Table A24 Width of a slit

Appendix B
Answers to Problems

Chapter 5

1 CALCULATIONS FOR DIFFERENT CODES

CODE	X	Y	CALC. VALUE
3	51	4	204
1	25	13	38
2	8	34	−26
5	4	3	64
4	62	5	12.4

Chapter 7

1 RADIUS = 443.334 M

2 SIDES OF TRIANGLE CM

A	B	C	ANGLE DEG	AREA SQ CM
17.2	9.8	14.1		69.1
	74	98	125.4	2955.7
292		405	30.5	30010.7
10.3	15.6		69	75

3 VOLUME OF CYLINDER = 111.33 CUBIC CM

VOLUME OF HEXAGONAL BAR = 103118 CUBIC CM

VOLUME OF CUBOID = 155.8 CUBIC CM

Chapter 12

1 Cos 30° = 0.866025   (to five terms)

2 REAL ROOTS :   − .24   AND   −2.76
   COMPLEX ROOTS
   COINCIDENT ROOTS :   4
   REAL ROOTS :   .85   AND   −2.35
   REAL ROOTS :   −1   AND   .33
   COMPLEX ROOTS
   COINCIDENT ROOTS :   − .5

3 WIDTH OF SLIT = 6.75E-2 CM

4 Slope = 0.1096
   Coefficient of correlation = 0.9953
   Young's modulus = $1.92 \times 10^{11}\, Nm^{-2}$

5 The answer will vary slightly depending upon the selection of random numbers but should be close to 11.1 weeks.

6 Monthly repayments = 156.97 and 209.29, respectively.

Appendix C
ASCII and CHR$ Codes

This appendix shows you what characters will appear if you PRINT CHR$ (X), for all possible values of X. It will also show the values obtained by typing PRINT ASC ("x") where x is any character you can type. This is useful in evaluating the character received in a GET statement, converting upper/lower case, and printing character-based commands (like switch to upper/lower case) that could not be enclosed in quotes.

PRINTS	CHR$	PRINTS	CHR$	PRINTS	CHR$	PRINTS	CHR$
	0		16	SPACE	32	Ø	48
	1	CRSR ↓	17	!	33	1	49
	2	RVS ON	18	"	34	2	50
	3	CLR HOME	19	#	35	3	51
	4	INST DEL	20	$	36	4	52
WHT	5		21	%	37	5	53
	6		22	&	38	6	54
	7		23	.	39	7	55
	8		24	(	40	8	56
	9		25	)	41	9	57
	10		26	*	42	:	58
	11		27	+	43	;	59
	12	RED	28	,	44	<	60
RETURN	13	CRSR →	29	—	45	=	61
SWITCH TO LOWER CASE	14	GRN	30	.	46	>	62
	15	BLU	31	/	47	?	63

PRINTS	CHR$	PRINTS	CHR$	PRINTS	CHR$	PRINTS	CHR$
@	64	U	85	◜	106	◣	127
A	65	V	86	◝	107		128
B	66	W	87	□	108		129
C	67	X	88	◨	109		130
D	68	Y	89	◩	110		131
E	69	Z	90	□	111		132
F	70	[	91	□	112	f1	133
G	71	£	92	●	113	f3	134
H	72	]	93	□	114	f5	135
I	73	↑	94	♥	115	f7	136
J	74	←	95	□	111	f2	137
K	75	⊟	96	◿	117	f4	138
l	76	♠	97	✕	118	f6	139
M	77	◫	98	○	119	f8	140
N	78	⊟	99	♣	120	SHIFT RETURN	141
O	79	□	100	▯	121	SWITCH TO UPPER CASE	142
P	80	□	101	♦	122		143
Q	81	◳	102	⊞	123	BLK	144
R	82	◧	103	▨	124	CRSR	145
S	83	◩	104	‖	125	RVS OFF	146
T	84	◿	105	π	126	CLR HOME	147

PRINTS	CHR$	PRINTS	CHR$	PRINTS	CHR$	PRINTS	CHR$
INST DEL	148	CYN	159		170		181
	149	SPACE	160		171		182
	150		161		172		183
	151		162		173		184
	152		163		174		185
	153		164		175		186
	154		165		176		187
	155		166		177		188
PUR	156		167		178		189
CRSR	157		168		179		190
YEL	158		169		180		191

Appendix D
Screen and Border Colour Combinations

You can change the screen and border colours of the VIC anytime, in or out of a program, by typing

POKE 36879, X

where X is one of the numbers shown in the chart below. POKE 36879, 27 returns the screen to the normal colour combination, which is a CYAN border and white screen.

Try typing POKE 36879, 8. Then type CTRL ![WHT key] and you have white letters on a totally black screen! Try some other combinations. This POKE command is a quick and easy way to change screen colours in a program.

				BORDER				
SCREEN	BLK	WHT	RED	CYAN	PUR	GRN	BLU	YEL
BLACK	8	9	10	11	12	13	14	15
WHITE	24	25	26	27	28	29	30	31
RED	40	41	42	43	44	45	46	47
CYAN	56	57	58	59	60	61	62	63
PURPLE	72	73	74	75	76	77	78	79
GREEN	88	89	90	91	92	93	94	95
BLUE	104	105	106	107	108	109	110	111
YELLOW	120	121	122	123	124	125	126	127
ORANGE	136	137	138	139	140	141	142	143
LT. ORANGE	152	153	154	155	156	157	158	159
PINK	168	169	170	171	172	173	174	175
LT. CYAN	184	185	186	187	188	189	190	191
LT. PURPLE	200	201	202	203	204	205	206	207
LT. GREEN	216	217	218	219	220	221	222	223
LT. BLUE	232	233	234	235	236	237	238	239
LT. YELLOW	248	249	250	251	252	253	254	255

Appendix E
Screen Codes

SET 1	SET 2	POKE	SET 1	SET 2	POKE	SET 1	SET 2	POKE
@		0	U	u	21	*		42
A	a	1	V	v	22	+		43
B	b	2	W	w	23	,		44
C	c	3	X	x	24	—		45
D	d	4	Y	y	25	.		46
E	e	5	Z	z	26	/		47
F	f	6	[		27	Ø		48
G	g	7	£		28	1		49
H	h	8	]		29	2		50
I	i	9			30	3		51
J	j	10	←		31	4		52
K	k	11	SPACE		32	5		53
L	l	12	!		33	6		54
M	m	13	"		34	7		55
N	n	14	#		35	8		56
O	o	15	$		36	9		57
P	p	16	%		37	:		58
Q	q	17	&		38	;		59
R	r	18	'		39	<		60
S	s	19	(		40	=		61
T	t	20	)		41	>		62

SET 1	SET 2	POKE	SET 1	SET 2	POKE	SET 1	SET 2	POKE
?		63		T	84			106
		64		U	85			107
♠	A	65		V	86			108
	B	66	○	W	87			109
	C	67	♣	X	88			110
	D	68		Y	89			111
	E	69	♦	Z	90			112
	F	70			91			113
	G	71			92			114
	H	72			93			115
	I	73	π		94			116
	J	74			95			117
	K	75	SPACE		96			118
	L	76			97			119
	M	77			98			120
	N	78			99			121
	O	79			100		✓	122
	P	80			101			123
●	Q	81			102			124
	R	82			103			125
♥	S	83			104			126
					105			127

Appendix F
Screen and Colour
Memory Locations

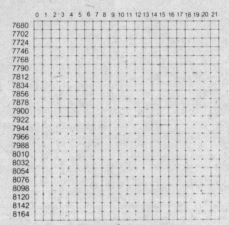

Screen location codes

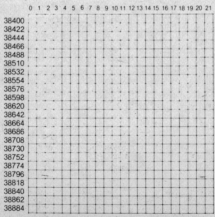

Equivalent colour location codes

Appendix G
Musical Scales

Note	POKE value	Note	POKE value
C	131	C'	193
C#	138	C'#	196
D	145	D'	200
D#	151	D'#	203
E	157	E'	206
F	162	F'	209
F#	167	F'#	211
G	172	G'	214
G#	177	G'#	216
A	181	A'	218
A#	185	A'#	220
B	189	B'	222
		C''	224

Note: ' = one octave higher; '' = two octaves higher.

Appendix H
Further Study

'Personal Computing on the VIC 20' (*beginner's guide*)
 Commodore, 675 Ajax Avenue, Trading Estate, Slough,
 Berks, England.
'VIC Learning Series' (*cassette & workbook materials*)
 Commodore, 675 Ajax Avenue, Trading Estate, Slough,
 Berks, England.
'VIC Revealed' (*advanced techniques*)
 Computabits, 41 Vincent St, Yeovil, Somerset.
'VIC Programmer's Reference Guide' (*advanced techniques*)
 Commodore, 675 Ajax Avenue, Trading Estate, Slough,
 Berks, England.
'PET Interfacing' (*control & laboratory applications*)
 Howard W Sams, 4300 West 62nd St, Indianapolis,
 Indiana, 46268, USA.
'Commodore Club News' (*magazine*)
 Commodore, 675 Ajax Avenue, Trading Estate, Slough,
 Berks, England.
'VIC Computing' (*magazine*)
 Printout Publications, P.O. Box 48, Newbury, England.
'Home and Educational Computing' (*magazine*)
 P.O. Box 5406, Greenboro, NC 27403, USA.

Index